The Religious Revolt Against Reason

The Religious Revolt Against Reason

by

L. HAROLD DeWOLF

Professor of Systematic Theology
Boston University

GREENWOOD PRESS, PUBLISHERS
NEW YORK   1968

Dedicated to Daniel L. Marsh

and

All Other Builders of the
New Boston University School of Theology

Acknowledgments

Indebtedness is acknowledged to far more persons than can be mentioned by name.

My thought on these problems began in many long discussions of faith and reason over the desk of my father, Lotan R. DeWolf, and to him my debt is immeasurable.

To many teachers I owe much. Edgar S. Brightman, who was my major adviser in graduate studies and is now a colleague, has contributed in such innumerable ways as only men who have been privileged to stand in similar relationships with him can fully understand. The love of truth and the spirit of independent inquiry which he so generously encouraged have led me to criticize and reject some of his views, as I do in this work and elsewhere. But such differences have not in the least detracted from the warm friendship between us nor the high regard in which I hold him as philosopher, crusader for freedom and devoted lover of God. Nor will the differences conceal from the discerning reader the wider area of agreement.

To Philosophics Anonymous, an informal monthly discussion group in Newton, I am indebted for criticism of a rough preliminary essay which has become Chapter Two

Acknowledgments

in this book. Of that group, Paul S. Minear and Nels Ferré made especially valuable suggestions.

Walter G. Muelder, my colleague and dean, has read the manuscript and given criticisms of rare usefulness.

To Albert C. Knudson, my teacher in theology, my distinguished predecessor in the professorship which I now hold and my loyal friend, I am indebted beyond expression. He has given freely not only years of instruction and thoughtful counsel, but also a patient and detailed reading of manuscript which has removed many a rough spot in the style and thought of this work.

I am grateful to The Macmillan Company for permission to reprint the several quotations from *God and Man* by Emil Brunner, and to The American-Scandinavian Foundation for permission to reprint the several quotations from *Philosophical Fragments* and *Concluding Unscientific Postscript* by Søren Kierkegaard.

To Mrs. James V. Miller I acknowledge with thanks a secretarial task done with skill and painstaking care.

My wife has typed the entire final draft and given other help with the manuscript, in addition to a wealth of loyal encouragement and the invaluable aid of a well-ordered home where Christian love reigns.

L. HAROLD DeWOLF

Newtonville, Massachusetts

Contents

The Religious Revolt Against Reason

CHAPTER ONE

The Revolters and Their Predecessors

Our world is mortal. This ancient truth has now been re-captured by millions. For since Hiroshima our physicists have been speaking the language of the Apocalypse and many ears deaf to other voices have listened to the scientists.

Not only is every man infected from birth with the fatal disease of being human, but the race as a whole is vulnerable. Atomic warfare is only begun and bacteriological warfare yet unused. These and other methods of destruction may yet bring human life on earth to an untimely end. On the other hand, the end may come when the sun becomes a nova and, increasing its heat by a modest proportion, makes the ocean vanish in a cloud of steam and reduces all the earth's surface to a sea of bubbling lava. Again the sun may cool, as many other stars have done, and leave the earth frozen and lifeless from pole to pole. It may be that life here will even continue for millions of years until the slow processes of oxidation will have robbed the atmosphere of its life-giving substance and all that breathes will perish.

The end may be far off, but the possibility that, by reason of man's own folly, it may be near has drawn from many minds the acknowledgment that an endless continuance of human history upon earth is at least improbable. This discovery has rudely shocked a generation accustomed to the spurious faith in a worldly immortality of social influence and the belief in endless historical progress.

OUR SITUATION

It is even clearer that the whole order of society which we have long taken for granted may soon undergo revolutionary changes. In any country of the world the pattern of life a generation from now may be scarcely recognizable. Changes in social customs, economic relations, moral codes and political institutions follow one another at a bewildering and accelerating pace. The rise and fall of nations, the bombing of vast areas into an abyss of desolation, the loss of confidence in established authority, and the ever-present threat of a yet more destructive cataclysm have left multitudes adrift, without faith and almost without hope.

Men know today that they are living among high explosives. Yet they can find no way to defend themselves against one another without throwing fire around. Modern man is trapped by his own clever folly.

It has been our habit, when in trouble, to seek help from science. And little wonder! Science warms our homes, expands our range of communication and travel and reduces the hours of our toil. By surgery, sanitation and the wonder drugs, it extends the life span until in America the average now approaches the limit of years once reserved for the fortunate few. We have science to thank not only for many material blessings but also for its great aid in banishing superstitious fears, making possible the wide dissemination of knowledge and extending the areas of human understanding. So often we have turned to science for help and received what we asked and to spare, that it is natural now, facing the threat of universal chaos and death, that we should feel inclined again to call upon the wizards of the laboratory for rescue.

But alas! this time the scientists are not only incapable of rescuing us, but are bound in a terrible slavery, helplessly throwing fuel on the fire which threatens to consume themselves and all of us. Many a scientist wants to escape the necessity of devoting his talents to devising means of self-destruction. But the machines which he has helped to make seem to have refashioned human institutions in their own likeness. Now these vast mechanized industries and armies have reduced the individual to a mere cog, helpless to escape the relentless motion which crushes his soul and prepares the means of destroying his body as well.

These developments are viewed with dismay by the children of a scientific age. On every hand we confront urgent problems which science has produced or aggravated. We do want to keep the convenience, health, freedom and enlightenment to which our laboratories have contributed so much. But we should also like to avoid the sense of personal futility in the midst of colossal struggles for material power and the constant threat that the giant we have released may suddenly turn upon us the full fury of his newly devised horrors. We know now that science can be a veritable demon of destruction as well as an angel of mercy and light.

Some voices tell us that the scientists can yet guide us to security and freedom. But, they say, the science which is needed is not the technology of the laboratory. Rather, it is the social sciences which must save us. Our understanding and control of material things have outstripped our understanding and control of men and nations. We must speedily overcome this cultural lag and bring our knowledge of man and society to a level commensurate with our mastery of atoms and machines.

Unfortunately, a second glance will show that the social sciences, as well as the physical, are blind to the light we seek. They, too, are led about by the gigantic forces of our age, supinely serving friend and foe alike. A Hitler or a Stalin can use the instruments of social psychology, economics and sociology to control the very souls of vast multitudes as no man could have done a century ago. Social science, like physical science, gives knowledge. Knowledge is power. But this power can be used for good or ill.

Our basic problems are not problems of means but of ends. We do have the technical skills to achieve a free society or a totalitarian society, peace or war. But few persons have any clear conception of the ends which individuals or nations should seek. The men who hold the instruments of control seek ends which are mutually exclusive and self-contradictory. They want peace and at the same time special privilege. They seek international law but also would retain unlimited national sovereignty. The scientists are concerned with causal laws and hence can tell what is the instrumental x which will lead to many a resultant y. If only we could tell them what we want! They can hardly be blamed for not providing us with the right tools for attaining a result which is yet undefined.

In the midst of all this moral confusion stands the bewildered and helpless individual.

Since science is not capable of solving the universal and ultimate problems now confronting us, many people are turning again to religion. When all around us are the waves of a pathless and abysmal sea, we instinctively lift our eyes to heaven. We long for a glimpse of some fixed star by which to steer our course.

But sometimes no stars appear. Indeed, in many churches where men seek eagerly for some clear sign from eternity, they find the sky of faith no less confusing and uncertain than the stormy waves of which they are so weary.

One hot summer night on a sudden impulse I went, with a companion, for a midnight swim off the South Shore of Massachusetts Bay. Leaving our automobile at the edge of the sand, we ran quickly down the beach and plunged into the water. The phosphorescence was so

bright that every dip of the hand produced a circle of flash-
ing gems and every breaker looked like a cascade of fire-
works. To ride the waves beyond the breakers we went
out some distance from shore. Then turning toward land
again I was suddenly gripped by a strange fear. All lights
on shore were out and all I could see were the shifting,
restless, ever-changing patterns of blue-green light in the
water. Instinctively I looked up from all this fascinating,
eerie confusion, for a view of the quiet stars. But then I
was seized by a new unearthly dread. From horizon to
horizon the sky was filled with an amazing display of the
northern lights, in colors matching those of the luminous
ocean. I was now at the center of a universe of weird, blue-
green forms, where all was moving and nothing was established.

The momentary panic I felt at Humarock Beach was
like the nameless, paralyzing fear which underlies much of
the feverishness apparent among men today. They could
stand the confusing changes of the world, if only heaven
would guide them. But the church to which they turn
seems to reflect the fascinating but deadly change and confusion of earth.

To be of service to the people in any period religion has
to relate itself to the problems and interests of the time.
But it must offer bearings independent of the current relativities. While addressing itself to our own age of science,
has religion lost its own essential message and become a
mere echo of this mortal world? The conviction has been

growing that many leaders in the Church have so far accommodated their message to the language and methods of contemporary science that they have lost the power either to enlighten or to encourage a generation which has more science than it knows how to manage, but which has lost faith.

In our time Christian leaders, apart from various intermediate positions, offer two radically opposed attitudes. Some have adopted the techniques and discoveries of the scientists and are making such changes in their religious teaching as this procedure requires. This is the path taken by the pragmatic modernists and naturalistic humanists. Their critics say that in so doing they have made of faith a mere reflection of the world's uncertainty and have become blind leaders of the blind. The radical alternative offered is for the men of faith to resist the encroachments of science in the field of religion by circumscribing some area of doctrine belonging to faith, and declaring its truth and value to be guaranteed by revelation and hence independent of all the tides and fortunes of human criticism and historical accident. This has been the procedure of the fundamentalists, the crisis theologians and various other proponents of what is broadly termed neo-orthodoxy.

One characteristic of the present neo-orthodox movement is the tendency of many representatives to repudiate in theology not only the specific methods and results of science, but human reason in all its forms. Probably no living theologian can be properly designated, without qualification, as an irrationalist. But on the other hand, many living theologians reveal a frequently recurrent and profound distrust of reason.

This distrust of reason in recent religious thought is the subject of the present study. The limited scope of the undertaking should be noted. The purpose is not to make a critical examination of the whole neo-orthodox movement, nor of the dialectical theology, nor of the thought of any one man. A general evaluation of the many-sided work of Reinhold Niebuhr, Emil Brunner, Karl Barth or Søren Kierkegaard would lead far beyond the limits of this volume. Attention will be concentrated here on one trend of thought and one only, namely, the tendency to doubt the right of reason to judge between truth and error in affirmations of Christian belief. In some of the men studied it would be easy to discover contrary trends, and all of them have brought forth many other teachings of great importance and value. For the purpose of combining some thoroughness with brevity these varied and inviting fields of exploration are left to other adventurers. Like many another specializing prospector we shall occasionally discover other precious metals besides those of which we are in search. But these will be by-products of our main task. This task is simply the description, analysis and critical evaluation of the irrationalistic trend in recent theology, especially in Kierkegaard, in whom it is most thoroughly developed, and the drawing of some conclusions from this study.

However, limited as it is, let no one be deceived as to the importance of our task. The methods to be used in religious thought are likely to determine the conclusions reached. The meaning of every article of faith, for both theory and practice, will be deeply affected by the reader's conclusions on the problems studied here. Let it be remembered that the ideas to be examined are offered by their defenders as means of escaping the confused relativities of our age. Some of these men are persons of great ability, knowledge and influence. They say that by following their example we can discover eternal landmarks of faith independent of all the uncertain change, confusion and peril of human thought and experience. Such a claim coming from such men in such a time merits the most thoughtful examination.

The procedure will be as follows:

In the remainder of Chapter One we shall first observe some general characteristics of the revolt against reason as represented in various contemporary writings. Then it will be noted that the roots of the movement extend far back into the history of Christianity, indeed into the New Testament itself. However, it will be noted that there are developments of theological irrationalism which are peculiar to the present age and that these new developments are largely due to the critical work of Søren Kierkegaard.

In Chapter Two we shall examine in some detail those objections to dependence on reason in theology on which the current distrust of reason is based. This examination will be both sympathetic and analytical. The aim will be to give the clearest possible view of the full strength and relevance of the Kierkegaardian charges against reason.

Chapter Three will be devoted to a point-by-point defense of reason against the charges.

In Chapter Four reason will take the offensive and present countercharges against the current irrationalism in religion.

In Chapter Five an attempt will be made to suggest ways by which those positive values for the sake of which the attacks on reason have been launched, may be conserved while at the same time the losses incurred when the authority and disciplines of reason are depreciated may be avoided.

THE REVOLTERS

Religion and reason have been often wedded, often divorced. Despite many announcements proclaiming their quarrels ended in lasting harmony, their peace has again and again been shattered by angry charges and recriminations.

We are living now in a period especially marked by estrangement and conflict. That a great new wave of irrationalism has been surging across the world of religious thought since World War I, no one acquainted with the theology of this period can doubt. The distrust of reason shows itself in many forms and in many degrees of emphasis and consistency.

The man who has done most to publicize and encourage this tendency in the second quarter of the twentieth century is undoubtedly Karl Barth. In method of exposition Barth is much more systematic, and in that sense rational, than many other living theologians. But when he is asked for proof of the doctrines he expounds, or the validation of faith itself, he appeals only to the authority of Christ, the Bible or the Church, or rather all three together. But how do we know that these are authoritative? Must not the Christian faith in the Church, the Bible and Christ be justified before the world in the language of universal reason or philosophy? Barth's answer is implied in most of his writings and explicitly stated in many passages. It is made especially clear and emphatic in *Credo*:

> Further, it is forced down my throat that the Dogmatic theologian is under the obligation to "justify" himself in his utterances before philosophy. To that my answer is likewise, No. Dogmatics has to justify itself only before God in Jesus Christ; concretely, before Holy Scripture within the Church. . . . It cannot be otherwise than that Dogmatics runs counter to every philosophy no matter what form it may have assumed. . . . All our activities of thinking and speaking can have only a secondary significance and, as activities of the creature, cannot possibly coincide

with the truth of God that is the source of truth in the world. The value of what theology has to say is measured by no standard except that of its *object*. . . . The question of the "proper" language of theology is *ultimately* to be answered only with prayer and the life of faith.[1]

How, then, will faith be defended against skeptical attack, if not by rational argument? Barth answers,

> But there has never been any other effective apologetic and polemic of faith against unbelief than the unintended one (impossible to intend! purely experiential!) which took place when God Himself sided with the witness of faith.[2]

For many years the name of Karl Barth has been linked with that of Emil Brunner. Although since 1929 they have been in sharp conflict on some issues, they have nevertheless continued to think alike on many matters. Moreover, while their dispute has shown Barth to be the more thoroughgoing in his rejection of reason, yet he and Brunner are agreed in proclaiming that by means of it men can attain no knowledge of God. Their position is well described by John Baillie:

> The idea of the total corruption of human nature, strongly entrenched in orthodox Protestantism but

[1] *Credo*, 185-186.
[2] *The Doctrine of the Word of God*, 31.

lately fallen into disrepute, was now not only vigorously reaffirmed by both writers, but was given an application even more extended than orthodoxy had usually given it; this total corruption being made so to cover the human reason as to render men incapable of reaching any knowledge of God by the exercise of their own powers of thought, or even of bringing them to a point in their thinking such as would enable them to welcome the Christian revelation, when it came, as answering a question they had already raised or meeting a need they had already felt. The Word of God in Christ came "vertically from above" into the existing human situation and appeared only as foolishness to the best of human wisdom. It did, indeed, meet with a response from those elected to respond to it, but this response was not on the ground of anything already present in their souls; rather did the revelation create its own response.[3]

Brunner regards the attack on philosophical method in theology as a fundamental purpose of the movement with which he identifies himself. He declares,

It is perhaps not unfitting to describe the theological movement of the present time as one which is con-

---

[3] John Baillie, "Introduction," in *Natural Theology*, comprising *Nature and Grace* by Emil Brunner and *No!* by Karl Barth, tr. by Peter Fraenkel.

cerned to take the Biblical concept of God seriously,
and by so doing to free it and our whole interpretation
of life from the stranglehold of Greek philosophy, in
which it has been stifled for thousands of years.[4]

If it be supposed that it is only Greek philosophy which
is to be opposed in theology, Brunner warns:

As all natural human action reveals the sinful heart,
so all philosophical speculation, when left to itself,
bears witness to the obscuration in the inmost recesses
of our reason. For this cause it is impossible to build
up the Christian proclamation of the Gospel and its
theology on the basis of a philosophical doctrine of
God.[5]

Philosophy, as he uses the term, "should be taken to
mean the possibility of a knowledge of God by means of the
reason."[6] Brunner's strictures against philosophy are to be
understood, therefore, as objections to the belief that any
method of reason can lead to a true knowledge of God.
God can be truly known only by special revelation.

The God of the Bible has nothing to do with the
philosophical concept of God, because he is not

[4] *God and Man*, 38.
[5] *Ibid.*, 40.
[6] *Ibid.*, 41 n.

thought as idea, but apprehended in his historical revelation of himself.[7]

It is just this provoking characteristic of being a contingent fact of history which distinguishes the Word of God from a truth of reason.[8]

The place conceded to reason in theology seems to increase as Brunner moves from one writing to another. His concessions to the rationalists are especially noteworthy in *Revelation and Reason*. But they have not erased the influences of his earlier, more extreme utterances.

Although in recent years Barth and Brunner have been the men most prominently identified with the repudiation of a rational theology, the radical distrust of reason has deeply affected many other theologians also. Especially have we learned to expect emphatic expressions of it whenever we talk with Protestant theologians from the Continent of Europe. But the trend has by no means been confined to the Continent. Barth has had a wide influence in Great Britain. So strong is the irrationalistic tendency there that at the Royal Society, commemorating the twenty-fifth anniversary of the British Institute, Viscount Samuel, president of the Institute, indicated as "the most urgent task of today, the task of countering what has been called 'the revolt from Reason' which has done such immeasurable

[7] *Ibid.*, 54.
[8] *Ibid.*, 123.

harm to this twentieth century."[9] Even in America, where the awful devastation of the bombings in World War II was not experienced, where the social atmosphere is much more optimistic and faith in human worth and power remains generally at a high level, irrationalistic expressions have become frequent among theologians.

Some of the most conspicuous evidences of the revolt in America are, quite naturally, to be found in the writings of avowed adherents to the theology of crisis. For example, Walter Lowrie's book, *Our Concern with the Theology of Crisis*, is full of firmly asserted unresolvable paradoxes and denials that rational criticism should be admitted as competent in matters of faith.[10] Similar, but more moderate and carefully phrased objections to rational method appear in the writings of such men as Paul Minear, Paul Lehmann, David F. Swenson and Douglas Horton.

But the influence of the revolt has extended much further and may now be found in the works of many thinkers who could hardly be regarded as crisis theologians. Of course, objections to philosophy and to intellectual criticisms of religious doctrines and literature have always been popular among unlearned religious people in America. But the present revolters are to be found even among the most learned men, thoroughly versed in the traditions of liberal philosophy.

It would be hard to think of an American theologian whose utterances are more widely read and discussed today

[9] See *The Hibbert Journal*, Vol. XLV, No. 2 (January, 1947), 178. The words quoted are those of the reporter, S. H. Mellone.

[10] E.g., see p. 150.

than are those of Reinhold Niebuhr. His own irrationalistic statements are counterbalanced by a broad dependence on philosophy, much skilled and cogent reasoning, and frequent concessions to the claims of rational theology. However, even the concessions are sometimes accompanied by claims which seem to deny them flatly, while Niebuhr's love of unresolved paradoxes and his dramatic attacks on the depravity of man's reason certainly have had the effect, among persons most influenced by him, of weakening confidence in rational processes and turning the edge of every critical objection to theological dogmas, however obscure or inconsistent. Perhaps the most clear and representative statement he has made concerning reason in theology is in his work on *The Nature and Destiny of Man*:

> Though the religious faith through which God is apprehended cannot be in contradiction to reason in the sense that the ultimate principle of meaning cannot be in contradiction to the subordinate principle of meaning which is found in rational coherence yet, on the other hand religious faith cannot be simply subordinated to reason or made to stand under its judgment. When this is done the reason which asks the question whether the God of religious faith is plausible has already implied a negative answer in the question because it has made itself God and naturally cannot tolerate another.[11]

[11] Vol. I, 165-166.

The specific argument here made against the right of rational criticism will be elaborated and evaluated later.[12] But now the question must be asked: If religious faith "cannot be in contradiction to the subordinate principle of meaning which is found in rational coherence," then is it not clear that a faith which does contradict reason is not a valid faith? And if this is true, should not religious faith be "made to stand under its judgment"? Which are we to accept, the admission that a true religious faith must be rationally coherent or the assertion that religious faith must not be subjected to rational evaluation? Such perplexing questions arise concerning much current theological writing, where the irrationalistic influence has left its mark but has not been able to dislodge the rational heritage of the long-established habits of critical thought.

A similar lack of confidence in rational evaluations of religious doctrine is evident in the thought of Nels Ferré. In his book *Faith and Reason*, Dr. Ferré stoutly defends reason and philosophy against the aspersions now being heaped upon them. In this connection he insists that philosophy, when it is soundly critical and firmly coherent, is an altogether valid and useful approach to truth.[13] But when he begins to define the meaning and value of theology, he insists that it is distinguished from philosophy by a difference of method. For "philosophical application is rational; theological, existential."[14] Moreover, although he

[12] See pp. 60 ff. and 100 ff.
[13] See especially p. 28.
[14] P. 142.

has insisted that both philosophy and theology are altogether valid, he finds that on some of the most basic issues their different methods drive them to contrary conclusions. In such instances he would apparently accept the theological solutions.[15] What, then, has become of the philosophical validity? Have we here a doctrine of double truth or of knowledge concerning different levels of reality? Or sheer unresolved paradox? In any event the "rational" method of philosophy is evidently subordinated to an "existential" theology.

In preparation for national and international conferences of seminary students in 1947 and 1948, and for the organizing Assembly of the World Council of Churches in 1948, there was published a series of highly stimulating volumes known as "The Interseminary Series." On the whole, the many contributors expressed less of the irrationalistic trend than was appearing in most exchanges of thought among theologians at the time. However, there are occasional evidences of it. Of these the most sustained and extreme occurs in the essay by John Knox entitled "The Revelation of God in Christ."[16] Dr. Knox endeavors to show that the principal doctrines of the Christian faith, including belief in God, immortality and the kingdom of God, not only cannot be convincingly supported by philosophical arguments, but are only made to look less credible when such "proofs" are attempted. We should, therefore, learn from

[15] See pp. 188-189, 192-193, 199.
[16] "The Interseminary Series," Vol. 3: Kenneth Scott Latourette, ed. *The Gospel, the Church and the World*, 3-25.

the example of "the first Christian generation." They frankly admitted that their message was "foolishness," and "then went out to prove that this foolishness was the foolishness of God and was wiser than men's wisdom."[17] In the next paragraph he declares,

> A religious faith which can be proved does not deserve to be believed—ceases indeed to be a religious faith at all. . . .[18]

It would have been helpful if it had been explained why the early Christians were to be commended because they "went out to prove" that their faith was "wiser than men's wisdom" and yet "a religious faith which can be proved does not deserve to be believed." Dr. Knox must have had in mind different kinds of proof, but they are not defined nor explained.

Similarly confusing is his conclusion concerning immortality. He says,

> Such a belief when one confronts the stark reality of death is, in the light of ordinary reason, incredibly absurd and fantastic. And none of the facile apologias for the belief, which we are so fond of making, succeeds in doing more than to remind the reflective reader or hearer of its rational implausibility. And yet

[17] P. 6.
[18] P. 7.

what sense does the world make, what meaning can
be found in human life and history without it?[19]

The last sentence is clearly an appeal to the criterion of
coherence or all-round reasonableness, that is to say, of
reason in the form both the commonest among plain people
and the most widely appealed to by critical philosophers.
This condemning of "ordinary reason," followed immediately by an appeal to the commonest form of reason, is
especially confusing since again no definitions nor explanatory distinctions are offered. The net effect, so far as
reason in religion is concerned, is at one and the same time
to disparage the use of rational criticism in theology and
to provide another example of irrational paradox.

This contemporary distrust of reason is especially striking
in an age characterized by marvelous achievements of rational discovery. The remarkable influence of irrationalism
among educated men today is largely due to the critical and
literary genius of its greatest modern proponent, Søren
Kierkegaard. A study of the modern revolt against reason,
and particularly of the religious revolt, must consequently
be devoted principally to a study of his ideas. Kierkegaard,
in fact, presented a critique of reason at once so bold and
so penetrating as to be unmatched in the history of Christendom. In addition he gave to this critique a literary expression of extraordinary vividness and persuasive power.

Many a recent reader of Kierkegaard's strange but bril-

[19] Pp. 8-9.

liant works has found in his defiance of reason an attitude which seemed altogether novel. There is no denying the creative genius of his thought. On the other hand, the partial or complete rejection of reason as arbiter of truth in theology is in principle as old as rational theology itself. Such rejection has appeared usually as a reaction to rationalistic attacks on religion.

Many men who have been recognized masters of reasoned knowledge have attacked sharply the faith of their contemporaries. From Xenophanes and Epicurus to Karl Marx and John Dewey, they have compelled the priests and devotees of religion to fight for their beliefs or to yield them. But the defenders of the faith have often been no less hostile to those who have dispassionately approved than to those who have ardently attacked their creeds. Religious apologists have sounded the alarm, not only when they have discovered a declared enemy, but likewise when they detected in the professed friend an air of condescension. For not only has the hollow wooden structure of a professed philosophical defense proved, on occasion, to be a Trojan horse well-manned with heretical ideas dangerous to the established faith, but even when devoid of such heresies it has threatened to lure religion into its own confines, there to live the restricted and anemic life of a prisoner. The religious man confronting the philosopher is as willing to be attacked as to be patronized.

A philosophical defense of Trinitarian dogma may be as heartily opposed as a militant atheism. Thus, in 1834, a

Tübingen professor, Adam K. A. Eschenmayer, published a book devoted in its entirety to a violent polemic against Hegel's "defense" of Christianity. Eschenmayer was not alone in believing that in defending Christianity Hegel had so radically reinterpreted it and so completely subordinated it to principles peculiar to the Hegelian philosophy as to make of his purported defense an actual attack.

When confronting the betrayers or open enemies of religious faith, theologians employ three main stratagems.

First, they often argue that reason is on the side of faith. Although the foes of religion appeal to reason they are accused of relying on fallacious arguments, of overlooking important evidence or of interpreting too narrowly the meaning of rational proof. Thus, an anonymous writer of the mid-nineteenth century wrote a book called *The Irrationalism of Infidelity*. The method is more ably represented by innumerable recent works under less obvious titles. A good example is Edgar S. Brightman's *Nature and Values* in which the author argues persuasively that a thorough examination of experience reveals evidence that theism is a more reasonable explanation of the facts than is naturalism.

A second mode of defense is to employ the first method of appeal to reason for support of some religious doctrines while insisting, at the same time, that there are other truths guaranteed by revelation but beyond the power of human reason to discover, understand or validate. Such doctrines are usually held to be in no opposition to reason, but only beyond it. They are to be accepted, therefore, on the authority of the Bible, the Church or mystical intuition. Thus Thomas Aquinas endeavored to give rational demonstration of the existence of an all-wise God, but he accepted the doctrines of the Trinity and the creation *ex nihilo* as revealed truths beyond the reach of human reason. The cosmological and teleological arguments proved, he believed, that God was the first and final cause of the universe. But no rational argument could prove that there were three Persons of one substance in the Godhead, nor that the world was created out of nothing by divine fiat. Yet he was assured of these doctrines by the authority of the Bible and of the Church.[20]

In some instances, a third, more daring stratagem is used. Not only is it admitted that some doctrines of the true faith are beyond all possibility of being proved or even fully grasped by reason. It is further conceded, and even aggressively proclaimed, that some true commitments of faith are radically contrary to reason. At the same time it is insisted that this contradiction of faith by reason is due not to the falseness of faith, nor even to the ineptness of this or that human thinker, but to the fundamental invalidity of reason in the realm of religion.

The second type of defense often tends to pass over into the third. For it is maintained in both that in some areas of religious doctrine, at least, reason is incompetent to serve

[20] Cf. the position taken by Swami Akhilananda in *Hindu Psychology*. For an able defense of an epistemology making room for the nonrational supplementation of reason, see Richard Müller-Freienfels, *Irrationalismus*.

as arbiter between truth and error. The distinction between
the contention that doctrine is beyond reason and that it
is contrary to reason is often difficult to maintain in practice.
For many defenders of the faith do not make clear what,
precisely, is implied by their delimitation of reason. Indeed,
it is difficult to see how they could be expected to do so.
If certain doctrines are beyond the bounds of human rational understanding, then it is obviously impossible for
reason to define precisely their relations to its own realm.
Moreover, when the usefulness and legitimacy of rational
criticism in any matter has once been denied, the obligation to employ in regard to it exact definition and faithful
consistency is not likely to be effectively acknowledged.
The process of indoctrination will require some pedagogical
precision and consistency, to be sure. But these may be
more verbal than real. Whenever an embarrassing critical
question is pressed, a way of escape is at hand, for the problem can always be thrown out of the court of rational discussion as a divine mystery. Roman Catholic writers on the
Trinity and on transubstantiation afford many examples of
such procedure, despite their vigorous defense of rational
method in theology.

Many other theologians, too, who do not fully reject the
validity of rational criticism do often join with the irrationalists in disparaging critical method. Though not properly classified as irrationalists they do at such times give aid
to the revolt against reason.

This revolt lacks the definiteness and consistency which
would be expected of any rationalistic position. Irrational-

ism is, naturally, an irrational trend, not a systematic epistemology. Throughout most of Christian history it has appeared only as an occasional expression of religious feeling or an *ad hoc* device of apologetics. It was not until the nineteenth century that it found an advocate who made of it a lifelong theme and carried the revolt into the camp of philosophy by the internal criticism of reason itself. Yet when Kierkegaard appeared he was able to strike many a cord already made familiar by irrationalistic utterances from a long line of distinguished predecessors.

ORIGINS

Kierkegaard and his disciples have frequently cited supporting evidence from the very source of the Christian religion in the New Testament itself. Whether Jesus or the apostle Paul ever rejected reason as a means of learning or testing truth about God and salvation will be considered later.[21] But however that may be, there are certainly passages from their recorded utterances which have encouraged such rejection. For the present, two will serve as examples.

> Jesus declared, "I thank thee, Father, Lord of heaven and earth, that thou hast hidden these things from the wise and understanding and revealed them to babes."[22]

[21] See pp. 102-105, 133-137.

[22] Matt. 11:25. All quotations in English from the New Testament will be given according to the Revised Standard Version of 1946, except as otherwise indicated.

This statement suggests not only that revelation has followed channels other than those best known to the wise, but even that Jesus and the Father positively favored "babes" in preference to the wise. What, then, become of men's earnest efforts to discipline their reasoning powers and to think rightly concerning divine things?

When Paul met criticism of his doctrine from learned men, he retorted,

> Where is the wise man? Where is the scribe? Where is the debater of this age? Has not God made foolish the wisdom of the world? For since, in the wisdom of God, the world did not know God through wisdom, it pleased God through the folly of what we preach to save those who believe. For Jews demand signs and Greeks seek wisdom, but we preach Christ crucified, a stumbling-block to Jews and folly to Gentiles. . . .[23]

The antirational force of such passages is emphasized the more by contrast with the praise of wisdom so frequently found in the Old Testament.

Such repudiations of worldly wisdom were echoed again and again as the Early Church struggled to maintain and extend its doctrine against the entrenched prestige of its adversaries. Did the trained teachers of Judaism reject the scriptural evidence of the gospel? That was part of God's plan to destroy their authority so that men might learn to

[23] I Cor. 1:20-23.

obey God rather than men. Did philosophers look on the Christian world view with scorn? Their contempt only served to fulfill the prophecies of the New Testament, so authenticating the Christian faith, and warning all Christians against the dangers of accepting instruction from men who prided themselves on their own wisdom rather than on the power and love of God. Did heretics appeal to reason against orthodoxy? By so doing they showed themselves to be children of pagan philosophy, not of Christian revelation.

Thus, in the second century, Tatian, whom Étienne Gilson calls "the prototype" of the Christian "enemies" of philosophy,[24] berated the Greek philosophers, both collectively and individually, with the most scathing denunciation and contemptuous ridicule.[25] It is worth noting, however, that Tatian did not altogether renounce human reason as an instrument of religious knowledge and judge of its truth. Rather, he appealed to reason in support of Christian doctrine, and denounced the wisdom of the Greeks as "contrary to reason."[26] It was not so much philosophy as Greek philosophy which he condemned. Indeed, he called the Christian position "our philosophy,"[27] and styled himself "Tatian, a disciple of the barbarian philosophy."[28]

More famous and thoroughgoing is the irrationalism of

[24] Étienne Gilson, *Christianity and Philosophy*.
[25] See his *Address to the Greeks*, especially chaps. 1-3 and 25-26.
[26] *Ibid.*, chap. 26.
[27] *Ibid.*, chap. 31.
[28] *Ibid.*, chap. 42.

Tertullian, who was much influenced by Tatian. Tertullian wrote of the heresies,

> These are "the doctrines" of men and "of demons" (I Tim. 4:1) produced for itching ears of the spirit of this world's wisdom: this the Lord called "foolishness" (I Cor. 3:18,25), and "chose the foolish things of the world" to confound even philosophy itself. For [philosophy] it is which is the material of the world's wisdom, the rash interpreter of the nature and the dispensation of God. Indeed heresies are themselves instigated by philosophy. . . . Unhappy Aristotle! who invented for these men dialectics, the art of building up and pulling down; an art so evasive in its propositions, so far-fetched in its conjectures, so harsh in its arguments, so productive of contentions—embarrassing even to itself, retracting everything, and really treating of[29] nothing! . . . From all these, when the apostle would restrain us, he expressly names *philosophy* as that which he would have us be on our guard against (Col. 2:8). . . . Away with all attempts to produce a mottled Christianity of Stoic, Platonic, and dialectic composition! We want no curious disputation after possessing Christ Jesus, no inquisition after enjoying the gospel![30]

Yet, like most other inveighers against philosophy, Tertullian, too, was quite willing to use philosophy when it

[29] Or settling (*tractaverit*).
[30] *On Prescription Against Heretics*, chap. 7.

served his purposes.[31] Indeed, he appeared at times to belong to the class of those who regard revelation as supplementing and not opposing reason. Sometimes the two views of reason were curiously entangled in his works. His main interest was apologetic. But he elevated a method of practical apologetics into a cognitive principle, declaring that reason was valid when it favored the gospel, but invalid when in opposition.

> One may no doubt be wise in the things of God, even from one's natural powers, but only in witness to the truth, not in maintenance of error; [only] when one acts in accordance with, not in opposition to, the divine dispensation. For some things are known even by nature: the immortality of the soul, for instance, is held by many; the knowledge of our God is possessed by all.[32]

Tertullian believed that the world was fundamentally rational, but warned,

> Divine reason . . . lies in the very pith and marrow of things, not on the surface, and very often is at variance with appearances.[33]

[31] E.g., note his references to Zeno and Cleanthes in his *Apology*, chap. 21. See also *Against Marcion*, I, chaps. 11-13. Cf. Adolph Harnack, *History of Dogma*, II, 231-236, especially 233, n. 1.

[32] *On the Resurrection of the Flesh*, chap. 3.

[33] *Ibid.*, chap. 3.

As a consequence he thought the human mind to be incapable of knowing the true, divine reason of things without the aid of special revelation from God.

Tertullian's lifelong tendency toward irrationalism grew more radical after he became a heretical Montanist. It is commonly believed to have been in this late period of estrangement from the Church that he wrote his most famous paradoxical passage:

> The Son of God was crucified; I am not ashamed because men must needs be ashamed *of it*. And the Son of God died; it is by all means to be believed, because it is absurd.[34] He was resurrected from the grave. It is certain because it is impossible.[35]

Since the main task in hand is not historical, mere mention can be made of the occasional outbursts of irrationalism in the usually systematic, logically constructed thought of Augustine, the contrasting of rational or philosophical and revealed or theological truth in the work of Averroes, or the strains of irrationalism in St. Bernard, Duns Scotus and William of Occam. Time must be taken, however, to see how the distrust of reason entered Protestant thought, especially through Luther and Calvin.

[34] *Ineptum.* Perhaps *foolish* or *inept* would convey the meaning better than *absurd*. It is questionable whether he ever said the words so often attributed to him or to Augustine: *"Credo quia absurdum"* ("I believe because it is absurd"). They are not in any of his extant works. However, that they do accord well with one of his often expressed sentiments is beyond doubt.

[35] *On the Flesh of Christ*, chap. 5.

LUTHER AND CALVIN

In this matter Martin Luther owed much to St. Bernard and Duns Scotus, whose works he read faithfully. According to the view which he developed, philosophy has its own domain, and in that it is valid. But it has nothing to do with religion.

> Philosophy understands naught of divine matters. I don't say that men may not teach and learn philosophy; I approve thereof, so that it be within reason and moderation. Let philosophy remain within her bounds, as God has appointed, and let us make use of her as of a character in a comedy; but to mix her up with divinity may not be endured.[36]

Luther goes further. Unregenerate human reason not only is incapable of discovering theological truth; it actually opposes the truth. Accordingly, Luther asks,

> Why do Christians make use of their natural wisdom and understanding, seeing it must be set aside in matters of faith, as not only not understanding them, but also as striving against them?[37]

Yet, he insists, once the soul is regenerated by faith it becomes capable of employing reason to good effect. Re-

[36] Hugh T. Kerr, *A Compend of Luther's Theology*, 4.
[37] *Ibid.*, 4.

plying to his own question why Christians use "their natural wisdom and understanding," he says,

> Answer: The natural wisdom of a human creature in matters of faith, until he be regenerate and born anew, is altogether darkness, knowing nothing in divine cases. But in a faithful person, regenerate and enlightened by the Holy Spirit, through the Word, it is a fair and glorious instrument, and work of God: for even as all God's gifts, natural instruments, and expert faculties are hurtful to the ungodly, even so are they wholesome and saving to the good and godly.
>
> The understanding, through faith, receives life from faith; that which was dead, is made alive again; like as our bodies, in light day, when it is clear and bright, are better disposed, rise, move, walk, etc., more readily and safely than they do in the dark night, so it is with human reason, which strives not against faith, when enlightened, but rather furthers and advances it.[38]

John Calvin is certainly no irrationalist in any thoroughgoing sense. The carefully reasoned arguments of his great system are justly famous. He regards reason as a most valuable instrument of faith. Moreover, he grants to reason, even apart from faith, the power to know some truth about God. However, this knowledge is not knowledge in the most proper sense of the word.

[38] *Ibid.*, 4-5.

We cannot with propriety say, there is any knowledge of God where there is no religion or piety. . . . What benefit arises from the knowledge of a God with whom we have no concern? Our knowledge of God should rather tend, first, to teach us fear and reverence; and, secondly, to instruct us to implore all good at his hand, and to render him the praise of all that we receive.[39]

The knowledge of God which we need, the knowledge of Him proper to a creature, is a knowledge which induces subjection to Him in reverent obedience. If we do not know that He is such a being as we must obey, we do not have real knowledge of Him.

Vain, therefore, is the light afforded us in the formation of the world to illustrate the glory of its Author; which, though its rays be diffused all around us, is insufficient to conduct us into the right way. Some sparks, indeed, are kindled, but smothered before they have emitted any great degree of light. Wherefore the Apostle . . . says, "By faith we understand that the worlds were framed by the word of God";[40] thus intimating, that the invisible Deity was represented by such visible objects, yet that we have no eyes to discern him, unless they be illuminated through faith by an internal revelation of God.[41]

[39] *Institutes*, I, ii, 1, 2.
[40] Heb. 11:3.
[41] *Institutes*, I, v, 14.

46

Furthermore, human reason as corrupted by sin is not only inadequate to provide a saving knowledge of God, but is a positively perverting influence.

> For as soon as a survey of the world has just shown us a deity, neglecting the true God, we set up in his stead the dreams and phantasms of our own brains; and confer on them the praise of righteousness, wisdom, goodness, and power, due to him.[42]

This charge of idolatry hurled by Calvin against the philosophers of religion has been repeated many times in the nineteenth and twentieth centuries, especially by the more radical of the Kierkegaardians. It will be elaborated and evaluated later.

However, before beginning the detailed account of the many charges currently made against the reliability of reason in theology, it is needful to give some attention to the man who introduced most of them into modern thought, and who gave to the theological attack against the authority of reason its most penetrating and persuasive form.

SØREN KIERKEGAARD

Wherever the distrust of reason is conspicuous in recent theology the reader is almost sure to find the name of Søren Kierkegaard. Walter Lowrie and David F. Swenson, who have been mentioned as crisis theologians prominent

[42] *Institutes*, I, v, 15.

in the revolt, are the principal translators of Kierkegaard's works into English, and both are devoted disciples. British and American thinkers not directly dependent on Kierkegaard but influenced by the crisis theology are usually readers of Barth and Brunner, both of whom derived their antirational bent largely from him.[43]

Karl Barth's dependence on Kierkegaard is too general and too well known to need extended comment here. When Barth is charged with "imposing a meaning on the text [of the Epistle to the Romans] rather than extracting its meaning from it," he declares significantly,

> My reply is that, if I have system, it is limited to a recognition of what Kierkegaard called the infinite qualitative distinction between time and eternity, and to my regarding this as possessing negative as well as positive significance.[44]

Brunner, as regards his distrust of rational approaches to God, points to Kierkegaard as his only modern predecessor who has expounded his own specific view:

> As all natural human action reveals the sinful heart, so all philosophical speculation, when left to itself, bears witness to the obscuration in the inmost recesses of our reason. For this cause it is impossible to build

[43] Cf. Paul Lehmann, *Forgiveness*, 197.
[44] Barth, *The Epistle to the Romans*, Preface to the Second Edition.

up the Christian proclamation of the Gospel and its theology on the basis of a philosophical doctrine of God. It was Kierkegaard alone among the great men of later times who had a firm and vital hold of this truth.[45]

More recently, Brunner has written,

> Since [the Reformation] the question, To what extent should the relation between reason and revelation be one of war or peace? has never ceased to occupy Protestant theology. Twice the solution of a radical antithesis has been suggested, first by Søren Kierkegaard, and secondly, under his influence, in the Dialectical Theology.[46]

Again, he says, "If anyone has ever used the slogan *credo quia absurdum*, it was Kierkegaard."[47]

Reinhold Niebuhr cites Kierkegaard's ideas and writings with conspicuous frequency and usually with approval. Occasionally he lavishes on him such high praise as he rarely bestows on any modern writer. In *The Nature and Destiny of Man*, Niebuhr refers to Kierkegaard oftener than to any other writer since the Reformation. He calls him "the greatest of Christian psychologists."[48] He says,

[45] *God and Man*, 40.
[46] *Revelation and Reason*, 310.
[47] *Ibid.*, 376.
[48] Vol. I, 44 n.

"Kierkegaard's analysis of the relation of anxiety to sin is the profoundest in Christian thought."[49] More significantly, revealing an important source of his own favorite irrational paradox, Niebuhr writes, "Kierkegaard's explanation of the dialectical relation of freedom and fate in sin is one of the profoundest in Christian thought."[50]

Nels Ferré, in *Faith and Reason*, makes many specific references to Kierkegaard, usually with favorable comment. More important is the evidence in his fundamental conception of theology. The Kierkegaardian influence appears clearly in his contrast between the "objectivity" of philosophy and the "subjectivity" of theology, and between the "rational" method of philosophy and the "existential" method of theology.

There is good reason why Kierkegaard should be so frequently given direct or indirect acknowledgment by men who express doubts concerning the competence of reason in theology. Not only is he historically the first of the crisis theologians, but his attack on the authority of reason in religion is more varied in appeal and better equipped with internal criticisms of philosophical method than any other which has ever been launched by a Christian thinker.

Søren Aabye Kierkegaard was born on May 5, 1813, in Copenhagen, and there he died on November 4, 1855.

[49] Vol. I, 182 n.
[50] Vol. I, 263. Niebuhr does think that Kierkegaard's irrationalism goes too far. For, says Niebuhr, "The final truth about life is always an absurdity but it cannot be an absolute absurdity." *Ibid.*, Vol. II, 38.

During his forty-two years he went abroad only three times, each trip being to Berlin. His fertile imagination took the place of travel, and provided him with such a varied and sensuous language as to bear more resemblance to the romantic essayists than to the theologians. His writing has the fascination of brilliant figures and penetrating thought, while at the same time it often tries the reader's patience with its devious prolixity and morbid preoccupation with sin and sorrow. On the other hand, he can be a model of conciseness, as in many passages of *Philosophical Fragments*; and frequently, as in his *Edifying Discourses*, he dwells on the love and mercy of God with childlike simplicity and trust.

Those who would understand Kierkegaard should read one of the two biographies by Walter Lowrie.[51] There they will learn of his unhappy childhood under the domination of a father whom he loved but who taught him that he and his family were under the curse of God because he had committed the unpardonable sin, and who in many other ways stamped him with a morbid outlook often approaching if not actually becoming a psychopathic condition.[52] As the reader observes the tragic family quarrels, the relatives who fell into insanity, his strange and pathetic love

---

[51] *Kierkegaard* and *A Short Life of Kierkegaard*.

[52] Kierkegaard himself writes, "I am in the deepest sense an unfortunate individual, who from the earliest time has been nailed fast to one or another suffering, to the very verge of insanity, which may have its deepest ground in a discordance between my soul and my body." Quoted by Lowrie, *Kierkegaard*, 47.

affair, his extreme vanity and self-pity,[53] and the unrestrained bitterness of his attacks on the clergy in Copenhagen, the temptation may arise forthwith to dismiss all that he wrote as the work of a disordered mind. But that would be a grave mistake.

Whatever a psychiatrist might say about the state of mind from which issued all the great quantity of Kierkegaard's writings, the thoughts he expressed have had a vast and yet increasing influence in philosophy and theology. Many men whose sanity is exemplary find in his writings the highest wisdom. Moreover, even in a wildly disordered dream a man may see the true solution of a problem. The psychological motivation of an utterance is neither proof nor disproof of the ideas expressed. That Kierkegaard wrote some profoundly searching criticisms of reason, as well as much else of great importance, will be apparent to any intelligent person who reads his books with an open mind.

Kierkegaard's consuming purpose was to bear witness to man's need of God and to God's all-sufficient grace. This he did by an extraordinary variety of writings which represent three stages in a great dialectic. As in Hegel's dialectic, one level of thought, or of life, after another is elaborated, shown inadequate and transcended. However, he rejects the lower levels rather than including them, as did Hegel,

[53] E.g., he writes, "When my poet comes he will assign me a place among those who have suffered for an idea; he will say about me: 'The martyrdom which this author suffered was due to the fact that he was a genius living in a market town.'" Quoted by David F. and Lillian M. Swenson in the Introduction to their edition of *Edifying Discourses*, Vol. II, xx.

in more comprehensive syntheses. Whereas Hegel resolved his antinomies, Kierkegaard rejected all synthetic solutions and insisted on absolute commitment to God in a faith which scorns the contradictions of all human thought. Thus, while Hegel is the philosopher of both-and, Kierkegaard is the author of *Either/Or*.

The first level which he subjects to examination is the aesthetic or sensuous. In *Either/Or, Repetition, Fear and Trembling,* and *Stages on Life's Road,* he seeks to represent in its most appealing forms the life of the man who lives for material satisfactions, however artistic and sophisticated, and to show the self-defeating character of such a life. Many intelligent men seek to escape the contradictions and baseness of such a life by the rational construction of a moral philosophy and the effort to live by it. Hence, in *Philosophical Fragments* and *Concluding Unscientific Postscript,* Kierkegaard endeavors to represent the philosophical mind at its best, making a critical examination of its own task and method.

In all these works he employs pseudonyms, as is fitting, since in them he is expressing points of view which he does not share, even though he is doing so in order to reveal their complete failure. He writes under his own name only in some specifically religious writings, published chiefly, though not exclusively, after the others had been completed.

It is not the purpose of this work to examine the whole of Kierkegaard's thought but only his charges against reason in theology, found principally in the two philosoph-

53

ical works representing the second stage of his dialectic. Moreover, the object of this study is not to be primarily biographical nor historical. Principal attention will not be focused on the relation of his irrationalism to the other aspects of his thought and life, nor on the specific historical sources and influences of his critique of reason. The task of the succeeding chapters will be rather to make the strongest possible statement of the objections to reason in theology suggested by Kierkegaard and echoed by more recent theologians, and then to evaluate these charges and the distrust of reason to which they have led in many minds.

CHAPTER TWO

The Charges Against Reason

Many and serious are the objections made by Kierkegaard and other recent thinkers to the use of reason in determining the proper content of theology. The objectors have not often brought these accusations together in one place. Moreover, even when that has been done, as by Kierkegaard in his *Concluding Unscientific Postscript*, the method has been called, with peculiar appropriateness, "Unscientific," which is to say, unsystematic.

As a result, it has been difficult to see the objections in distinct outline and in their relations to each other. The defender of rational method is likely to feel that he is being shot at from behind every bush and tree without once having a fair view of the enemy against whom he fights. Likewise, many a revolter against reason as a decisive instrument in theology fails to recognize how many and relatively important are the arguments which have been advanced in support of his own position.

The analyst who would present these arguments in systematic form confronts serious difficulties. Not only have the various charges against reason been stated hitherto without precise differentiation, but they are inherently difficult to distinguish clearly. Nevertheless, they must be separated, as far as possible, if any clear evaluation is to be made.

At first the arguments will be presented without criticism, excepting only such questioning as may make possible the more effective releasing of their full force. Critical evaluation will be presented later.

However, before unleashing the attack on reason it is necessary to define more specifically the objective of the assault.

DEFINITION OF REASON

What is the reason which is attacked? It is important to observe that it is not limited to the so-called rationalistic method of a Spinoza or Descartes. The object of criticism is not merely the effort to discover truth by doubting all which can be doubted and rearing on a foundation of indubitable axioms a structure of geometrically deduced philosophy. Nor is the specific critical method of a Kant or of the empirical sciences the "reason" which the theological irrationalists reject. Their position is much more radical than would be a criticism of one method by the defenders of another method through which human thought might search out the truth.

Kierkegaard has had no more appreciative and authoritative interpreter than David F. Swenson. It is he who writes as follows in a note on a passage in *Philosophical Fragments*:

> The thoughtful reader will already have noted that "Reason," as used in this chapter and throughout, is not to be taken in any abstract-intellectual sense, but quite concretely, as the reflectively organized common sense of mankind, including as its essential core a sense of life's values. Over against the "Paradox" it is therefore the self-assurance and self-assertiveness of man's nature in its totality. To identify it with any abstract intellectual function, like the function of scientific cognition, or of general ideas, or of the a priori, or of self-consistency in thinking, etc., is wholly to misunderstand the exposition of the *Fragments*. Specifically, Kant's distinction between Reason and Understanding, or any other similar distinction, is wholly beside the point.[1]

Similarly, Karl Barth declares,

> All our activities of thinking and speaking can have only a secondary significance and, as activities of the creature, cannot possibly coincide with the truth of God that is the source of truth in the world.[2]

[1] *Fragments* (New York: The American-Scandinavian Foundation), 99-100, note on chap. III, 39.
[2] *Credo*, 186.

In his book *Revelation and Reason*, Emil Brunner makes it clear that he does not now agree with Kierkegaard's absolute antithesis between reason and faith and consequent rejection of reason as instrument of theological knowledge.[3] However, when Brunner faces this problem he thinks of reason in similarly broad terms, as will be evident to anyone who reads the whole passage to which reference has just been made. Likewise, he has said in an earlier work, "By reason I mean not merely the intellect but all the faculties of man as such."[4]

On the other hand, Kierkegaard's rejection of reason as instrument of religious knowledge is not meant to imply that reason is of no use at all. He believes that outside of the crucial problems of existence, that is to say, the fateful questions of the ultimate faith by which man lives, reason is altogether legitimate. Moreover, even relative to faith the reason is granted some value. For

> the believing Christian not only possesses but uses his understanding, respects the universal-human, does not put it down to lack of understanding if somebody is not a Christian; but in relation to Christianity he believes against the understanding and in this case also uses understanding . . . to make sure that he believes against the understanding.[5]

[3] Pp. 310-311.
[4] *The Theology of Crisis*, 14-15.
[5] *Postscript*, 504.

58

The Charges Against Reason

Kierkegaard's declaration just quoted helps to answer one objection often made to his critique of reason. If he does not believe in reason, it is asked, then how can he use reason to criticize anything, even reason itself? To this objection two replies can be made in behalf of his procedure. First: human reason may be used to determine the limits of its own jurisdiction, even though not to determine the ways of God; and second: only by rational criticism can reason be criticized internally and hence in terms which would be persuasive to those in bondage to it. It should be recalled also that the Danish thinker, when he is using reason to criticize reason, writes under a pseudonym, as if to warn that he is making himself free to speak as much as he likes in terms not his own. So the apostle Paul matched the boastings of his opponents by some on his own account, but warned, "I speak as a fool." It is precisely one of Kierkegaard's greatest claims to fame that he was the first of all Christian theologians to make a sustained attack on reason, not merely from the religious standpoint of a dogmatic existentialist, but also from the theoretical standpoint of the rationalists themselves. He uses both standpoints freely, as will be seen in the analysis about to be undertaken.

For convenience the charges against reason will be divided into four classes, attacking respectively reason's objectivity, its presumption, its ineffectiveness, and the evil consequences of trust in it.

A. CHARGES AGAINST THE OBJECTIVITY OF REASON

Every textbook on scientific or philosophical method praises the virtue of objectivity. A man who is objective is emotionally free to follow the evidence wherever it may lead. He may be inclined to hope for one result rather than another. But if he is to make full and proper use of reason to gain valid results he must steel himself against all such inclinations.

If the disciple of reason is an astronomer, determining whether he has discovered a new planet or only a long-charted star unfamiliar to him, he may be hopeful that he will find that it is a planet and so establish his fame for ages to come. But he must fight against such an emotion and plot the course of the observed speck of light as precisely as if he cared for nothing but accuracy. Not by so much as a hair must he let his personal ambitions influence the recording of a single position on his chart.

If he be a physician diagnosing a disease of his own son, he will hope that the trouble is nothing serious, despite his contrary fears. But his diagnosis, being a rational procedure, must be objective if it is to be reliable. So the physician battles against the father within him. Not one bit of damning evidence must be overlooked or minimized, nor yet must the examiner lean over backwards, in combating his fears, so as to slight the more benign symptoms. Whatever storm of paternal concern may be raging in his breast, he must see to it that his eyes, fingers, ears, and above all his mind are only the physician's, observing as precisely and computing as coldly as if he were only physician and no man at all. This is sometimes too much to ask. Hence, even though he be an unexcelled specialist in the very type of disease he fears, when it is his own son who is the patient he may prefer that a colleague make the fateful diagnosis.

Consider, then, the case of the philosopher seeking to know whether he is immortal or whether there is a God to whom he owes allegiance. Such a man faces an ultimate question concerning his own eternal destiny. If he is to make legitimate and hence reliable use of his reason, he must be as detached in spirit as if he were an intelligence in some other universe, curiously inquiring whether that little creature, man, might have any important ·future awaiting him. In all this weighing of evidences, all this subtle balancing of value-judgments and sense perceptions, this facing of experiential data and the demands of systematic clarity, not by one iota must he allow his concern for his own soul to affect his thought. If he does he has lost objectivity and with it the reliability of his reason. But here arise the first charges against reason.

1. *That Objectivity Is Unchristian.* Cool detachment is very well in mathematics or astronomy. Even in medicine, though dealing with precious human life, such dis-

interestedness is acceptable and even praiseworthy, since it concerns, in practice, only the means to be chosen for attempting a humane ministration to which the practitioner is already committed. But our philosopher confronts a radically different problem. This problem has to do not with means but with ends, or rather *the end*. It concerns not merely the choice of a path to be taken toward a previously chosen goal, but the decision what goal to seek or even whether there be in all existence any goal or any meaning worth seeking. Here there is not a part of a man, say a physician or a philosopher, who can stand over against the man as man and subject all his fears and hopes to a passionless inquiry into questions of his eternal destiny. For the values of being a philosopher and all the principles and norms of philosophy itself are equally at stake when a man inquires about the God who, if He is God, is the ground of all norms and the source of all values.

If our philosopher be concerned about the existence of the God who speaks in the Bible and about the eternal life which is held before him there, he cannot be objective without having already in that objectivity turned his back on God. For the God who speaks in the Bible requires that a man give all to Him in love. "You shall love the Lord your God with all your heart, and with all your soul, and with all your mind, and with all your strength."[6] A man cannot commit all of his heart, soul, mind and strength to the love of God and have any part, aspect or moment of his

[6] Mark 12:30.

life uncommitted and so able to be objective about the existence, commands and promises of God.

Kierkegaard puts it this way:

> For an eternal happiness is rooted in the infinite personal passionate interest, which the individual renounces in order to become objective, defrauded of his interest by the predominating objectivity.[7]

Hence,

> Anyone who posits inspiration [of the Scriptures], as a believer does, must consistently consider every critical deliberation, whether for or against, as a misdirection, a temptation for the spirit.[8]

2. *That Objectivity Is Impossible.* Because it is so completely alien to the whole meaning and demand of Christianity, objectivity in considering the truth of Christianity, say the revolters, is not only unchristian; it is impossible.

Some philosophical problems do lend themselves to objective treatment. A philosopher can think coolly about eternal Ideas and wonder about their relation to the sun above him or the earth beneath. He may play dispassionately with syllogisms and seek out the logical relations between their terms and all their possible arrangements.

[7] *Postscript,* 28.
[8] *Ibid.,* 27. Cf. 19, 35-36, 42.

This is an altogether proper activity and may be a most pleasant one.

> All honor to philosophy, all praise to everyone who brings a genuine devotion to its service. To deny the value of speculation . . . would be, in my opinion, to prostitute oneself.[9]

The rejection of philosophy would be especially stupid, Kierkegaard points out, in a man who, like himself, is especially fond of the classical Greek thinkers.

> For he must know that Aristotle, in treating of what happiness is, identifies the highest happiness with the joys of thought, recalling in this connection the blessed pastime of the eternal gods in speculation.[10]

Yes, and the philosopher may objectively discuss divine things too, on condition that he be bound to think of divine things as Epicurus did. For Epicurus regarded the gods as having no relation to him, neither through having created him, nor through caring for him, nor yet through providing him with a life to come. A philosopher may speculate about one whom he calls God as objectively as any scientist discusses an eclipse of the moon, as a distant object of speculation in relation to which he is not involved in an infinite concern.

[9] *Ibid.*, 54.
[10] *Ibid.*

But for the speculating philosopher the question of his personal eternal happiness cannot arise; precisely because his task consists in getting more and more away from himself so as to become objective, thus vanishing from himself and becoming what might be called the contemplative energy of philosophy itself. . . . But the blessed gods, those great prototypes for the speculative philosopher, were not concerned for their eternal happiness; and so the problem did not at all arise in paganism. But to treat Christianity in the same manner is simply to invite confusion.[11]

For it is the human subject's own eternal destiny, capable of infinite qualitative differences throughout, the one all-inclusive object of infinite concern to him—it is that which he would investigate when he would investigate Christianity. If he is examining something in which he has not an infinite concern, something which leaves some part of him free of involvement, then he may be dealing with something interesting and something worthy of speculation, but he is not considering Christianity. When a philosopher professes that he is considering Christianity objectively in order to discover whether it is true, he may be misrepresenting his attitude, falsely claiming to be detached and dispassionate as he knows a philosopher must be if his thought is to be valid. This misrepresentation may be due either to self-deception, at which human beings are espe-

[11] *Postscript*, 54.

cially adept, or it may be due to a willful desire to deceive others. But in either case the objectivity is only a fiction if it is really Christianity with which he has to do. On the other hand, it may be that what he is calling Christianity is merely one of the innumerable speculative substitutes about which a man can be objective because they do not involve him in an infinite concern.

3. *That Subjectivity Is Superior to Objectivity*. There are some things which can be objectively known. By cool computation a geometer can know that the square on the hypotenuse of a right triangle is equal to the sum of the squares on the two sides adjacent to the right angle. By detached, systematic observation and disinterested thought a botanist can determine the classification of a rare flower. But what is love? No amount of objective study could find out what love is. The words of other persons who are said to know what it is may be copied but that is not to know what love is. The behavior of a young mother who loves her baby may be observed and duly noted with all the analytical detail so dear to the hearts of some psychologists. But a sigh, a lowered head, repeated movements of the lips, a quickened pulse, and expanded veins which redden the cheeks are not love. A person who had never loved even for a moment nor to a slight degree, could see and describe all of these. Yet he would not have the slightest inkling of what love is. On the other hand, the young mother, though

she never heard of psychology and is not troubled by any desire to be objective, knows at once.

What is by its nature impersonal can be known impersonally, which is to say, objectively. But what is by its nature personal can be known only personally, that is, subjectively. Objectivity is therefore fine for geometers, but for him who would know what love is, subjectivity is required.[12]

It is not alone the personal within oneself which is to be known only by subjectivity. It is anything truly and fully personal. I can learn not only what love is in myself by actually loving someone; it is also only by loving someone that I learn what love is in other persons.

However, all that has been said thus far is only introductory to what Kierkegaard would teach about the need for subjectivity in order to know the Christian's God. For while we may experience love, we cannot experience what it means to be God, even for a moment. Neither can we be like Him, so that by looking into some experience of our dependent, creaturely selves we can see what it is like to be God.

Sometimes a great poet must hardly know whether to laugh or to be angry when he has bared his soul and told of the vision and rapture from which his finest poem came, and then some miserable rhymester who scarcely knows a poem from the alphabet comes to him, gushing, and says, "I'm a poet too, and I know just how you felt." Yet between

[12] Cf. Brunner, *God and Man*, 67.

the rhymester and poet the distance is negligible as compared with the difference between a man and his Creator, who is "from everlasting to everlasting." What, then, has subjectivity to do with the knowledge of God?

Neither by objective speculation nor yet by the most ardent subjectivity can I know what God is to Himself. Only God can know what it is to be God knowing Himself. Yet I may, perchance, know what it is to be a man knowing his Creator. But if so it will be only by subjectivity.

Sometimes when I hold my smallest boy upon my knee, telling him of mysteries he never heard before, and when I see the wonder and trust in his eyes, I wonder at another mystery known to him but not to me. What is a loving father as a boy of four knows him? I do not know. No person can know objectively. Only the boy can know subjectively. Once I was four and had a father who loved me well. I presume that in those days I knew. But I cannot well remember now what he was to me then. I could know only by being the four-year-old son of such a father, by listening to him speak to me, and by looking up into his eyes with wonder and trust. Objectivity I have now in speculative moments as I ask what a father is to a small boy. But I have not the subjectivity of being the boy listening, wondering, loving and trusting.

Now it may not make much difference whether I know what a father is to a small boy or not, since I know what a father is to his son grown to maturity, and what a father is to himself, and what a boy is to his father. But when we are thinking of knowing God, we must remember that there is only one standpoint from which we can possibly know Him. That is the standpoint of a specific individual creature dependent on Him for existence and for eternal happiness, hence looking up to Him with infinite concern.

> The question cannot be how man in general and as such can know the Word of God. This question is objectless, for over against the Word of God there is no such thing as man in general and as such, but it is what it is by being spoken concretely to this or that man.[13]

To assume the air of a detached, unconcerned observer is to assume a falsehood at the start. I am only the creature which I am, and cannot know what God is to any other being than just such a creature. I must therefore know Him from the subjectivity of an infinitely concerned creature or not know Him at all. To be sure, I may assume toward Him the attitude of a rebellious, disobedient creature, infinitely concerned but with a sinfulness matching the concern. And if I do there is some hope that I may come to know Him. For in that event I am precisely what I purport to be, namely, an infinitely concerned, yet rebellious, sinful creature. But objectivity can lead me nowhere excepting away from God. For an unconcerned spectator I can never be.[14] Hence,

[13] Barth, *The Doctrine of the Word of God*, 224.
[14] Cf. Kierkegaard, *Postscript*, 50-52.

even he who is lost through passion has not lost so much as he who lost passion, for the former had the possibility.[15]

On the other hand, the rebellious man cannot truly know God excepting as he gives up the rebellion. The son who has a loving father but who will not love him, listen to him and trust him cannot learn what it is to know a loving father. Since he rebels against his father, he knows him only externally as the man who gives inconvenient commands, provides him with food and shelter, and grants to him occasional little luxuries. In short, he knows him only impersonally, in roles which someone other than his loving father might fill. Only by making himself veritably his father's child can the son really know his father.

Not by rebellion, much less by objectivity, can you know the truth about God. You may know only when you turn to God and yield yourself to Him in passionate, decisive faith. After that, any attempt at objective reasoning about His existence or the truth of His Word is a step backward, "for only the truth which edifies is truth for you."[16]

B. CHARGE OF PRESUMPTION

Archimedes is said to have boasted that with his newly discovered principle of the lever he could move the earth

[15] *Postscript*, 540. Cf. 485.
[16] Kierkegaard, *Either/Or*, II, 294. Cf. *Postscript*, 169-224.

itself, if only he had a fulcrum on which to rest the lever. Reason, too, requires a fulcrum. However weighty the evidence which a thinker may place upon one end of his argument, and however unbreakable the logical relations within the argument itself, the whole must rest upon a ground of postulation. There are various assumptions underlying different reasonings. The logical positivists have, in recent years, pointed out many of them. But among the assumptions underlying every argument, whether it concerns the stock market or immortality, is the assumption that reason itself is competent to deal with the matter in hand. Hence arises another objection:

That Supreme Faith in Reason Is Idolatry. There is no offense when a thinker believes his reason competent to decide whether eyestrain has been causing his headache. For he is assuming only that he is able to relate certain of his own experiences. Likewise, when he supposes that his reason can determine the relation between the diameter and circumference of a circle, there is no presumption, because he is only assuming jurisdiction of a human mind over its own concepts. But quite different, argue the Kierkegaardians, is the faith in reason shown by a philosopher who is trying to decide by reason whether God exists or whether he ought to fear and obey Him.

Here is a strange phenomenon. The man is trying to decide whether there exists a Being of such a nature that he ought to fear and obey Him as the Supreme Judge of all the world. If he can find out that there is such a God, then he will be obliged to obey Him above all others. Indeed, if He exists, there are no others worthy even to be heard in His presence. If He exists, then even now, while the philosopher considers whether He exists, the man who is considering whether God exists is already dependent upon God for his own existence and for the rightness or wrongness of his every thought. What authority does he seek, to tell him whether he should believe that the Supreme Authority of the universe exists? What judge does he call upon to decide concerning the Judge of all the earth whether He is to be believed in and obeyed or not? What majestic voice will be asked to speak from the heavens and give the word permitting or prohibiting this man to believe in and obey the God on whom all truth and right depend? What voice indeed? The man himself! Here he sits gravely asking his own reason whether he may be permitted to believe that God exists and should be obeyed!

Now suppose that his reason assents. Suppose that, rejoicing, he bows his head before the God whom his reason has given him leave to worship. Suppose that he proclaims to all men within hearing that he has learned that God exists and must be obeyed by everyone. But later some new ideas occur to him. Gravely he weighs the evidence again, and sadly finds himself commanded by his reason—which is to say by himself thinking—to cease worshiping God and even to stop believing that He exists. With heavy heart he bows to the decree. Who, then, was his deity? Who was the supreme authority whom he must obey even if obedience meant the denial of that One whom he had called God? Was it not his own reason?

If you would know, then, whom the philosopher of religion worships as his deity, as he weighs the evidence for and against theism, pay no attention to the direct testimony of his words. All the while, he is proclaiming, albeit indirectly, a more convincing testimony. He has a pantheon of deities, but its supreme member, the one who has power to make and unmake all the rest, is his own reason. That he must at all costs obey.

Any faithful loyalty is a beautiful thing to see, as loyalty. The philosopher's loyalty to reason often appears noble and heroic. For in obedience to it he will give up all else. Only when one remembers that this deity to whom he gives such allegiance as few give to their Creator is simply himself thinking, only then does the comic and yet tragic aspect of philosophy show itself. It is comic that the philosopher should cast his own shadow and then take it for his god. It is tragic that he should in this way miss the chance of knowing the God who, if He exists, must be supreme.

To allow reason to determine the content of religious doctrine is, then, a form of idolatry, the more ludicrous because in practicing it a man puts himself in the place of God. When this idolatry is practiced, others follow. For having begun to honor himself as the supreme divinity, then

With the well-known ambition of a devoted father, man decks the children of his self-assertion with the same authority with which he has previously decked himself. .... His conception of the world and thus his world become full of ideas and principles, points of view scientific, ethical and aesthetic, axioms, self-evident truths social and political, certainties conservative and revolutionary. They exercise so real a dominion and they bear so definitely the character of gods and godheads, that not infrequently devotion to them actually crystallises into mythologies and religions.[17]

C. CHARGES OF INEFFECTIVENESS

In view of the great accomplishments of human reason, especially since the Renaissance, it may seem strange that one charge against it should be that it is powerless to achieve its own purposes. The leading revolters are intelligent men of the modern world. They know well the brilliant successes of reason in the natural sciences. However, they insist that, as instrument of religious knowledge, reason is pathetically ineffective. Some of their most important charges are intended to support this contention.

1. That Reason Never Attains Certainty. When a lonely, confused, despairing person goes to church, he may hear the preacher say that there is a good God who loves him and will forever exercise a tender care for him. No

[17] Barth, *The Knowledge of God and the Service of God*, 18. Cf. Stanley R. Hopper, *The Crisis of Faith*, 35.

matter how disheartening his failures in business, how cruel the desertions of his friends, how enervating the ill-health of his advancing years, how brazen the sky above him, still God lives and He loves him. If only he could believe that! Everything would be different if he could take firm hold on that affirmation. Then, beyond the reach of all the disasters which could befall him as a sojourner on earth would be his truly unconquerable soul. He would be not merely stubborn in will, like the pitiful spirit of Henley's "Invictus," shouting defiance at the heavens while he goes down into annihilation, but truly unconquerable because firmly held by faith in the everlasting love of God.

Moreover, he does almost believe. He has the "will to believe." But some doubts assail him. When he wants most to rest all the weight of a heavy heart on the faith which the minister has proclaimed, he first tests it out as a carpenter tests the ladder which a young apprentice has placed for him, before he steps from the roof to its top rungs. As he puts a little weight of rational criticism on his new hope he feels it sway and slip uncertainly. He hastily steps back to make a new analysis of his situation. He senses clearly that his assurance of this new doctrine is not strong enough to bear him up. It must be more firmly braced so that no doubt can overthrow it. He wants to base his eternal happiness upon the sure knowledge of his teaching. Nothing less than certainty will be sufficient for this purpose. Certainty he must seek.

Feverishly he seeks evidence to support the belief he

would hold. He finds much. But soon he doubts the foundations upon which his arguments have been built. He must take more time and study the matter more thoroughly. He calls the thinkers of the ages to his aid. More and more evidence he discovers, and at ever deeper levels of thought. Yet always there is the lingering doubt about the accuracy of this bit of evidence or the truth of that presupposition. He has gone far, and if he can clear up only these few remaining difficulties, certainty will be his. Eagerly he presses on. But somehow he never arrives.

> There are indeed, in the objective sense, results everywhere, a superfluity of results. But there is no decisive result anywhere.[18]

The individual must not suppose that the trouble is merely with his own poor powers of thought. Let him not suppose that some philosopher with native genius and long training could solve the problem and arrive at the positive affirmation for which his own poor powers struggle in vain. For the failure is inherent in the very nature of human thought.

> The positive in the sphere of thought comes under the head of certainty in sense-perception, in historical knowledge, and in speculative results. But all this positiveness is sheer falsity. The certainty afforded by

[18] Kierkegaard, *Postscript*, 34-35.

sense-perception is a deception, as one may learn from a study of the Greek sceptics, and from the entire treatment of this subject in the writings of modern idealism, which is very instructive. The positiveness of historical knowledge is illusory, since it is approximation-knowledge; the speculative result is a delusion. For all this positive knowledge fails to express the situation of the knowing subject in existence. It concerns rather a fictitious objective subject, and to confuse oneself with such a subject is to be duped. Every subject is an existing subject, which should receive an essential expression in all his knowledge. ... He moves constantly in a sphere of approximation-knowledge, in his supposed positivity deluding himself with the semblance of certainty; but certainty can be had only in the infinite, where he cannot as an existing subject remain, but only repeatedly arrive.[19]

This impossibility of attaining certainty about existence by any rational method may be better understood if it be noted that reasoning must proceed from certain premises to conclusions. If the thinker is to be certain that his conclusions are true he must not only be sure that his inferences are valid but also that the premises with which he began are true. How is he to be certain of this? He must either prove the premises by further inference from other premises or he must find them given as data of experience.

[19] *Ibid.*, 75. Cf. Barth, *Doctrine of the Word of God,* 12.

If inference is made from other premises the problem is simply repeated. Eventually the inferring must begin with an arbitrary assumption, which would not be certainly known, or else with a premise given in experience. All possibility of rational certainty, then, rests on the possibility of gaining sure premises from experience of reality. Without troubling ourselves with the question whether any sort of proposition is ever given as true in experience, we need only note that our most convincing experiences often deceive us. We see objects which have all the appearance of reality and which we take to be real, only to learn later that we were dreaming. Even when awake we are subject to illusions, mirages, faulty memory and, perhaps, even hallucinations, so that things are often not what they seem.

Moreover, in thinking about God and immortality we can adduce as evidence only comparatively complex data requiring much interpretation before the conclusions can be reached. When a finite human being, subject to all the errors and self-deceits which are the common lot of man, supposes that he can by his own powers arrive at conclusions about God and his own eternal destiny, and that he can by such means know these conclusions with certainty, he must have forgotten what manner of being he is.

The rational quest for certainty invariably becomes, therefore, the pursuit of a will-o'-the-wisp. There are always a few more links to be supplied in the argument, and there is always the possibility that while searching for these he may come upon some new evidence of quite another kind.

Before he has found the links for which he went in search, the new evidence may have compelled him to revise his whole system. The search for truth is, indeed, as Kant said, "an endless task." Yet until it is finished the whole system of thought remains uncertain. The systematic philosopher

> says with speculative emphasis: "Not until we have reached the end of our exposition will everything become clear," . . . True, the dialectician is amazed to hear the same philosopher admit that the System is not yet completed. . . . In a scientific structure the absence of the conclusion has retroactive power to make the beginning doubtful and hypothetical, which is to say: unsystematic.[20]

The irony of it is that the more faith a man has in his reasoning processes the more he will feel bound to undertake this search for the rainbow's end. The more he is imbued with the scientific or philosophical spirit, the more he will insist that he must not believe until he is certain. Yet a candid criticism of his self-appointed task would show him that it is an impossible one. In fact, he often does see the impossibility more and more clearly as he goes along in his reasoning. Hence, the further he goes on the path which was to lead him into the blessedness of certainty, the further he finds himself from it. Thus John Dewey wrote, near the end of his book, *The Quest for Certainty*,

[20] Kierkegaard, *Postscript*, 16-17.

Man has never had such a varied body of knowledge in his possession before, and probably never before has he been so uncertain and so perplexed as to what his knowledge means, what it points to in action and in consequences.[21]

This much-advertised rational path to certainty might well be described in the words which Lewis Carroll put in the mouth of the Tortoise to describe a syllogism. For it turns out to be

a race-course, that most people fancy they can get to the end of in two or three steps, while it *really* consists of an infinite number of distances, each one longer than the previous one.[22]

2. *That Rational Certainty Would Be Fatal to Faith.* The dialectical theologians are not content to charge that reason can never achieve a sure knowledge of God; they insist further that the kind of certainty which reason seeks would not, if attained, support faith, but would destroy it.

It is characteristic of our whole earthly human life to be under tension. We are forever torn between opposing forces and contrary appeals. Security and peace are always just around the corner. A youth thinks that when he is

[21] Pp. 312-313. Cf. Irwin Edman, *Philosopher's Quest*, especially "Explanation of the Absence of a Conclusion," 273-275.
[22] Lewis Carroll, "What the Tortoise Said to Achilles," first published in *Mind*, December, 1894, and later in *Logical Nonsense*, 501. The argument of the whole essay is highly relevant.

grown, settled in his chosen occupation, and head of a family, his troubles will be over. The adult smiles indulgently, supposing that it is really the child who is free from care. Actually, he, too, is victim of the same fondness for seeking the sense of ease in the mere absence of the cares which now afflict him. He sees the child free from the anxieties which beset the head of a family, and forgets all the uncertainties, perplexities, loneliness and injuries which beset childhood and which are equally grave to the child. Likewise, the man, in his quest for security, looks ahead to the new house, the increase in salary, the new business deal he is about to complete, or perhaps the divorce and remarriage of which he has begun to dream. But security is always somewhere else. Each new problem solved reveals new ones more than sufficient to replace it.

It is in this situation of tension that the way is prepared for faith. The disciple of reason supposes that faith is a kind of knowledge. Therefore, the more certain the evidence he finds for the doctrines of Christianity the more steadfast and sure he thinks his faith will be. But "faith is not a form of knowledge."[23] "The conclusion of belief is not so much a conclusion as a resolution."[24] It is achieved "not by knowledge but by will."[25]

[23] Kierkegaard, *Fragments,* 50.

[24] *Ibid.,* 69.

[25] *Ibid.* Similarly, he says that "doubt can be overcome only by a free act, an act of will" (*ibid.,* 67). On the other hand, he says that "faith is not an act of will" (*ibid.,* 50). In this last statement he may mean that faith is not initiated by man's will and is not within man's power without God's having first contributed "the condition," i.e., the "Paradox" of the Atonement.

Faith is a passionate, decisive act. Now the kind of certainty for which the believer in reason seeks is conceived as a state of spiritual repose, a condition in which one could at last rest, assured that all would be well. But such security would be a dangerous foe to passion and hence to faith.

> While faith has hitherto had a profitable schoolmaster in the existing uncertainty, it would have in the new certainty its most dangerous enemy. For if passion is eliminated, faith no longer exists, and certainty and passion do not go together.[26]

Faith is a radical act. It has about it a kind of fanatical recklessness and violence, explosively banishing doubt. Jesus said concerning the kingdom of heaven that "men of violence take it by force."[27] A man who succeeded in finding security in the assured knowledge that all was well would not be capable of such revolutionary violence.

Accordingly, the Christian believer, even if he studies philosophy, does not base his faith upon it.

> Rather, he associates circumspectly with philosophy, lest it lure him away from the certainty of faith (which has in every moment the infinite dialectic of uncertainty present with it) so as to rest in an indifferent objective knowledge.[28]

[26] *Postscript*, 30.
[27] Matt. 11:12.
[28] *Postscript*, 53.

3. *That Doubt Is Caused by Sin and Cannot Be Cured by Reason.* It is commonly supposed that when a college youth begins to doubt the faith of his fathers, his questionings are caused by the new evidence which he confronts. He has become acquainted with some new theories of the natural sciences, or his readings in history contradict the teachings of the Church. Perhaps he has listened to a professor of philosophy who pointed out certain speculative objections to belief in God. Doubtless he has learned in sociology that the moral ideals of different peoples vary with their mode of making a living, and so he finds it hard to believe in one eternal Lawgiver who judges all mankind.

Doubt is not unknown in other areas of human instruction. Occasionally a child doubts that the earth is spherical. This is not strange because he can see that it is flat. Moreover, he observes that even a trained circus goat finds it difficult to stand on the top of a large ball, and for a man to stand on the under side of it would be out of the question, whereas men are reported to stand erect easily in all parts of the earth. Now when a child has such a doubt and such reasons for doubting, a good teacher will know what to do. Patiently he will show him that his evidences are not so good as he supposed and that other evidences prove convincingly that the earth is spherical after all. Doubts of reason must be answered by evidences appealing to reason.

The answer to the youth's religious doubt, therefore, seems obvious. Let a skillful teacher show him that none of the evidence from natural science conflicts with the religious doctrine he has learned in his childhood. Let the teacher show that some historians present views of history quite in accord with faith, that there are many philosophical arguments for belief in God and the objections have been powerfully answered by some of the greatest thinkers. Let the youth learn, too, that the varying moral ideals of **different peoples** are no evidences against the truth of one ideal any more than the many superstitions which have been held concerning the sun are proof that there is no truth about it which condemns all contrary notions as false. The student's doubt is caused by evidence. Very well, then, let it be cured by better evidence.

Here the revolters enter an emphatic objection. Doubt of the Christian gospel, they say, is not caused by evidence and cannot be cured by it. The youth's religious doubts are decked out in rational form but they are not rational in cause nor in their essential nature. If he had not gone to college he would have found other objections to the Christian life. They might have appeared less respectable intellectually, but they would have accomplished the same purpose of concealing from himself his sinful condition and so protecting his careless, selfish purposes from interference. If now you argue with him, you will learn that his doubts are not rational in motive. Give him all the theistic evidence you can. Call the greatest theistic philosophers to your aid and pile up the demonstration into the proportions of a landslide. Still the youth will find excuses for making no decisive commitment to God. He may become a clever theistic philosopher, and spend his life discovering new evidences for doubt and new methods of meeting those evidences. But no amount of reasoning will make of him an active Christian believer.

Says Kierkegaard,

> They would have us believe that the objections against Christianity come from doubt. This is always a misunderstanding. Objections against Christianity come from insubordination, unwillingness to obey, rebellion against all authority. Therefore they have hitherto been beating the air against the objectors, because they have fought intellectually with doubt, instead of fighting ethically with rebellion.[29]

The doubts cannot be cured so long as they are treated as rational in character. For they are actually produced by sin and are expressions of sinful pride. They are to be cured, therefore, by the only cure possible for sin, namely, faith. Confront the youth with the fact of his sinful pride and with the paradox of the God who is his Judge but who is also his dying Saviour and who requires of him a decisive, passionate commitment of his whole self to Him as the only way of salvation. If he then complains that he cannot understand why he should believe this, or even what it means

[29] Quoted from Kierkegaard's *Journal* by Walter Lowrie, in *Kierkegaard*, 187. Cf. *Postscript*, 485.

85

to believe this, let the minister who would overcome his doubt proceed

> with the passion of existential effort, . . . proclaiming that the paradox cannot and shall not be understood, . . . that the task is to hold fast to this and to endure the crucifixion of the understanding.[30]

When the believing friend who wants to establish the youth in faith is tempted to try answering the doubts by reason, let him be warned:

> If the proof could thus be produced, as doubt demands it, the doubt would no more be checked than illness can be healed by the medicine it desires. But on the other hand, if you wish to be convinced, then the apostle . . . directs you to the more perfect way, . . . for the word of faith would not fight doubt with its own weapons.[31]

Clergymen, in particular, must avoid being drawn into arguments about evidences for or against the doctrine they preach.

> The man who is called ought, according to divine ordinance, to·use his divine authority in order to be rid of all the impertinent people who will not obey,

[30] *Postscript*, 500.
[31] Kierkegaard, *Edifying Discourses*, Vol. II, 39.

but want to reason; and instead of that men have, at a single go, transformed the Apostle into an examinee who appears on the market with a new teaching.[32]

Kierkegaard would have it understood, once and for all, that no amount of rational apologetics can be of the slightest service to Christian faith.

The Christian cause is in need of no *defense*, it is not served by any *defense*—it is *aggressive*; to defend it is of all misrepresentations the most inexcusable— it is *unconscious crafty treachery*. Christianity is aggressive; in Christendom, as a matter of course, it attacks from behind.[33]

Briefly, the cause of doubt is not reason but sin. The cure of doubt is not reason but faith. Without faith reason is futile, for the sin of an unbelieving heart will corrupt reason to its own purposes. But when faith is present proof is unnecessary and unwanted. "Faith does not need it; aye, it must even regard the proof as its enemy."[34] Therefore, neither for the believing nor the unbelieving does reason have any value in the overcoming of doubt.

[32] Kierkegaard, "Of the Difference between a Genius and an Apostle," in *The Present Age and Two Minor Ethico-Religious Treatises*, 148.

[33] Back of title page of "Thoughts Which Wound from Behind—for Edification," in *Christian Discourses*, 168.

[34] *Postscript*, 31.

4. That Reason Cannot Comprehend Existence. Whenever a man thinks, the currency of his thought is conceptual. Everything which he attempts to describe or prove
must first be reduced to the terms of universals, just as a
farmer cannot put the value of his wheat or cattle in the
savings bank until he has first exchanged his goods for
money. Without a concept a man cannot think. But existence is always particular and hence always misrepre-
sented by concepts.

Josiah Royce, who was by no means skeptical of man's
rational powers, wrote a striking passage showing the difficulty, and even the impossibility of representing an actually existent individual by the terms of discourse. Royce
describes a young man who is in love and who wants to
tell what his beloved means to him. But whether he speaks
of her beauty, her loveliness, or the noble quality of her
spirit, he only places her in a class with other women who
are beautiful or lovely or noble. He succeeds in describing
a type of woman, but not the existing individual object of
his love. If his love be genuine, loyal love, then even though
several women were created so alike that he could not in
any manner describe the difference between them, yet he
would seek to find out which individual was the one whom
he loved and his love would remain perplexed and frus-
trated until he found her. For he loves an individual, not
a type. On the other hand, his descriptions can embrace
only a type and inevitably miss the individual.[35]

Now Kierkegaard argues that such difficulties are in-

[35] Josiah Royce, *The Conception of Immortality,* 30-40.

herent in all human thinking which seeks to grasp any existence other than the thought itself. For a man's reason deals only in his own thoughts. Here is a strange paradox. Reason, when engaged in its most serious business, seeks to comprehend what exists. But if it ever succeeded it would have become something other than reason, for it would then be entertaining a particular and not a concept. The thinker not involved in this paradox is saved from it only by being content to substitute his thoughts for reality. Hence

> the thinker without a paradox is like a lover without feeling: a paltry mediocrity. But the highest pitch of every passion is always to will its own downfall; and so it is also the supreme passion of the Reason to seek a collision, though this collision must in one way or another prove its undoing. The supreme paradox of all thought is the attempt to discover something that thought cannot think. This passion is at bottom present in all thinking, even in the thinking of the individual, in so far as in thinking he participates in something transcending himself. But habit dulls our sensibilities, and prevents us from perceiving it.[36]

All relations between existing beings are particular relations between particulars. Now a person's thought, in which he deals with universals, depends upon the position he occupies in that particular which is the whole of exist-

[36] *Fragments,* 29.

ence. For all thought is accomplished by particular individuals having particular standpoints. Philosophers of religion usually suppose that the worth of the individual depends on his relation to certain universal principles or moral laws. If he subordinates his individual acts and his whole individual life to the proper universals, then he is assured of God's favor. But actually no particular acts or persons can be properly evaluated by their relation to abstract principles, for the universal always misses precisely the most distinctive and important thing, namely, the individual existence. The universal ideals which are called moral laws are more or less accurate, though always inadequate, descriptions of certain kinds of existence. But such descriptions are always ex post facto. "All understanding comes after the fact."[37] On the other hand, only the particular existence has real value, and only in the relations of existent individuals to the whole of existence are the values actually generated which the laws so thinly portray. Hence,

> The paradox of faith is this, that the individual is higher than the universal, that the individual determines his relation to the universal by his relation to the absolute, not his relation to the absolute by his relation to the universal.[38]

[37] *Postscript*, 108.
[38] From *Fear and Trembling*, quoted by Lowrie in *Kierkegaard*, 264. Cf. *Postscript*, 315.

Salvation is, therefore, by a passionate individual commitment to God and unquestioning obedience to Him—an obedience which is not deterred by running counter to the laws of rational ethics. For God exists and He can save, but the laws are at best later, inadequate descriptions of existence, and hence have no power to save.

5. That Human Reason Cannot Find God, the Wholly Other. Again, it is contended that the reason of man cannot discover God, nor yet understand Him when He reveals Himself, because man can understand only in terms already found within himself, and God is unlike any and all of these. No concept is accurate, no analogy is appropriate, to represent God. For He is no part of the man who seeks to know Him. Since the man does seek to know Him, God must obviously be unknown to him. Since it is not the mere man himself whom the seeker has encountered in passion and now wishes to know, it must be another. Indeed, the Unknown is encountered as a completely different Being.

Now ordinarily, when we wish to know what is unknown, we attempt this by elaborating, extending or combining knowledge already possessed. This is all very well when we are merely analyzing and developing our own concepts, as in geometry. But now we are confronting a being not at all overlapping any part of ourselves or our ideas.

91

But because it is absolutely different, there is no mark by which it could be distinguished. When qualified as absolutely different, it seems on the verge of disclosure, but this is not the case; for the Reason cannot even conceive an absolute unlikeness. The Reason cannot negate itself absolutely, but uses itself for the purpose, and thus conceives only such an unlikeness within itself as it can conceive by means of itself; it cannot absolutely transcend itself, and hence conceives only such a superiority over itself as it can conceive by means of itself.[39]

Since God is unlike man, there follows

the further consequence, that if man is to receive any true knowledge about the Unknown (God) he must be made to know that it is unlike him, absolutely unlike him. This knowledge the Reason cannot possibly obtain of itself; we have already seen that this would be a self-contradiction. It will therefore have to obtain this knowledge from God. But even if it obtains such knowledge it cannot understand it, and thus is quite unable to possess such knowledge. For how should the Reason be able to understand what is absolutely different from itself?[40]

6. *That the Evil in Experience Is Incapable of Rational Explanation.* It is obvious that one of the influences

[39] *Fragments*, 35.
[40] *Fragments*, 36-37.

furthering the irrational trend in theology is the social chaos produced by two catastrophic wars. In a recent discussion, when an American thinker insisted that reason supported faith, a theologian from Europe retorted,

"That may seem plausible enough for you, protected and prosperous as you are. But if you had seen the world fall in on you, the forces of evil and destruction sweeping away everything on earth which you treasured, would your reason then conclude that a good God watched over the world and cared for His people? If, in such a cataclysm, you believed in God, would your belief be a reasonable inference from the observed evidence? Would it not be held rather in spite of the evidence, as an irrational paradox?"

It is not alone in the evil destruction wrought by man that a rational theism confronts grave difficulty. Even if a thinker looks only at nature, he may see so much of waste, cruelty and destruction that his rational inference is that Chance reigns over all.

The wisdom of God in nature, his goodness, his wisdom in the very governance of the world—are all these manifest, perhaps, upon the very face of things? Are we not here confronted with the most terrible temptations to doubt, and is it not impossible finally to dispose of all these doubts? But from such an order of things I will surely not attempt to prove God's existence; and even if I began I would never finish, and would in addition have to live constantly in suspense, lest something so terrible should suddenly happen that my bit of proof would be demolished.[41]

It is interesting to observe that some of the contemporary philosophers of religion who are most rationalistic in method nevertheless conclude that there is much in the world which is ultimately nonrational. Especially is this true of Edgar S. Brightman, who holds that there is much utterly purposeless or "surd" evil in the world. Such evil he would account for, not by attributing to it some meaning which we can but dimly discern or which is known only to God, but rather by charging its existence to a nonrational "Given" in the nature of God Himself.[42] In such a philosophy a rational method has finally arrived at an "explanation" in terms of the ultimately nonrational. But is not such a device actually an admission that not only human but even divine reason is unable to account for the facts? For if, as Dr. Brightman believes, the rational nature of God is the ground of all rational structure and hence of all valid inference, and if that rational nature of God is not metaphysically prior, but only parallel to the nonrational Given, then there is no *reason* why the nonrational Given should give rise to such and such results rather than others. Metaphysical explanation is thus thrown ultimately outside the bounds of reason, even the bounds of divine reason.

[41] *Fragments*, 33. Cf. Barth, *The Epistle to the Romans*, 49-50.
[42] Brightman, *Philosophy of Religion*, 240-341.

Kierkegaard, on the other hand, places less reliance on human reason because he trusts more fully the complete rationality of God. There is much in the world which man cannot fit into the system of rational purpose as he conceives it. On this Brightman and Kierkegaard are agreed. But from this proposition, Brightman concludes that these surd evils belong in no system, human or divine. Kierkegaard, on the other hand, concludes th_t here is another evidence that the reason of man, caught as he is in the temporal flux and all its existential involvements, is incapable of discovering the meaning which is nevertheless present in the refractory elements. He says,

> An existential system cannot be formulated. Does this mean that no such system exists? By no means; nor is this implied in our assertion. Reality itself is a system—for God; but it cannot be a system for any existing spirit.[43]

Brightman, then, constructs a system by which the greater part of experience and what he regards as its fundamental direction of movement can be accounted for in terms of God's rational will. The rest of the data he leaves without interpretation but excuses the failure of man to discover their meaning in the system by declaring them

[43] Kierkegaard, *Postscript*, 107. "Existing," as the context shows, here implies being in time, or *"in-der-Welt-sein"* (*Postscript*, Introduction by Walter Lowrie, xviii), as contrasted with the eternity and hence "finality" of God.

outside the system, even outside the system of God's own reason. They must constitute unfinished business for man's speculation because they are still unfinished business for God's good will.

Kierkegaard, on the other hand, refuses to believe that the true system of reality has been discovered while many of the data have to be excluded from it. He takes the requirements of rational coherence too seriously to believe that a rational metaphysics has been established so long as much of experience remains unsystematized. Since, in view of the existential flux in which a man stands or rather struggles, it is manifestly impossible for him to order everything in its proper place, he concludes that man's reason is incapable of giving an account of the world. Whereas Brightman sacrifices the complete rationality of God in order to defend the adequacy of human reason to explain everything which is in principle explainable, Kierkegaard defends the complete rationality of God by admitting the inadequacy of human reason, an inadequacy of which he believes he has found many other evidences also.

D. CHARGES OF EVIL RESULTS

The Kierkegaardians have criticized the objective spirit required by rational method, the proud presumption of reason and its ineffectiveness in accomplishing what it sets out to do. But the charges do not end here. For, it is said, while the men who trust in reason do not achieve by it the results which they set out to gain, they do produce a number of other consequences which are vicious.

1. *That Trust in Reason Substitutes Theory for Decision.* It was observed earlier that the task of reason is a very long and, indeed, an endless task. While this work of seeking evidence, analyzing, comparing, weighing, summing up, and revising goes on, the issue being studied remains undecided. Precisely this fact is said by Kierkegaard to be the most deadly result of putting one's trust in reason.

There is no objection to engaging in the endless task of speculation as speculation. It is a refined form of enjoyment and as such is inexhaustible, like some game of solitaire which can never be finished. But when speculation is taken as the guide of real living, then it becomes the foe of life. When a man leaves it to his reason to determine whether he will believe in God and commit himself decisively to Him, then all is lost. His reason will go on forever, arriving at various degrees of probability and approximation, but never at that degree of finality which is beyond all degrees because it is final decision.

> For it is very far from being true that the longer a man deliberates and deliberates, the nearer he comes to God; on the contrary, the truth is that the longer the deliberation becomes while the choice is postponed, the farther he removes himself from God. . . . To choose God is certainly the most decisive and the

highest choice; but "alas" for him who needs long deliberation, and "woe" unto him the longer he needs it. . . . The ungodly calmness with which the irresolute man would begin in the case of God (for he would begin with doubt), precisely this is insubordination; for thereby God is deposed from the throne, from being the Lord. And when one has done this, one really has already chosen another master, wilfulness, and thus becomes the thrall of irresoluteness.[44]

It will be observed that this evil consequence of trust in reason arises from two characteristics of reason previously noted, namely: (1) its requirement of objectivity or complete indecisiveness while the reasoning goes on, and (2) its inability ever to complete its task by arriving at intellectual certainty. Since the man who would use reason as his guide must withhold decision until reason's work is done, and since this work is never done, such a man is therefore required by the demands of reason never to make the decision. Since for the salvation of an existing person it is decision which is necessary, the result is that the man who trusts in reason is lost.

2. *That Dependence on Reason Leads to Pantheism.*
Among modern philosophers the one for whom Kierkegaard had greatest respect was Hegel. Indeed the Dane often

[44] *Christian Discourses*, 90. Cf. the story of Eudamidas and Xenocrates, related by Kierkegaard in *Postscript*, 34 n.

referred to Hegelianism simply as "the System."[45] Since he regarded the philosophy of Hegel as possessing both the best and worst characteristics of a metaphysics taken seriously, he could not help being impressed by its pantheistic character. Since every pantheism makes the individual man in some sense identical with God or at least a moment or fragment of His being, Kierkegaard viewed this aspect of "the System" with especially deep hostility. For he regarded God as wholly other than man and considered no sin worse than that idolatrous pride which leads a man to confuse himself with God. Moreover, a man will hardly come into a passionate encounter with a God of whom he himself is an aspect or moment, and it is only by confronting God in despairing subjection that a man can be saved.

However, it is not only in Hegel that Kierkegaard and other theologians influenced by him take issue with pantheism. For Kierkegaard regards every metaphysical system as implicitly pantheistic, even if it professes to oppose pantheism. He makes this point in the following passage:

> So-called pantheistic systems have often been characterized and challenged in the assertion that they abrogate the distinction between good and evil, and destroy freedom. Perhaps one would express oneself quite as definitely, if one said that every such system fantastically dissipates the concept *existence*. But we ought to say this not merely of pantheistic systems; it

[45] Note especially *Fragments* and *Postscript*.

would be more to the point to show that every system must be pantheistic precisely on account of its finality. Existence must be revoked in the eternal before the system can round itself out; there must be no existing remainder, not even such a little minikin as the existing Herr Professor who writes the system. But this is not the way in which the problem is usually dealt with. No, pantheistic systems are attacked, partly in tumultuous aphorisms which again and again promise a new system; and partly by way of scraping together something supposed to be a system, and inserting in it a special paragraph in which it is laid down that the concept *existence*, or actuality, is intended to be especially emphasized. That such a paragraph is a mockery of the entire system, that instead of being a paragraph in a system it is an absolute protest against the system, makes no difference to busy systematists.[46]

It will be noted that in this argument Kierkegaard's emphasis falls upon what he regards as the necessarily finished and hence static character of a systematic metaphysics, which precludes any place for the genuine freedom of an individual making real decisions in a changing world, and which therefore implies an all-inclusive monism or pantheism.

Emil Brunner is more direct and clear in his statement of a similar argument, but he emphasizes the coherent

[46] *Postscript*, 111.

unity implied by rational method, rather than the finality
against which Kierkegaard protests in the name of individual freedom and real change. Says Brunner,

> The fundamental conviction underlying every sys-
> tem is monistic. The metaphysician, whether he be
> the metaphysician in the narrower sense, or the specu-
> lative idealist, has the confidence that thought, and
> that means human thought, has the power to pene-
> trate to the ground, the unity of all things; conse-
> quently that this unity is present in the last resort in
> his own thinking; that the meaning and the coherence
> of the world discloses itself to his thought. In his
> thought he has the infallible access to that unity or
> ground or ultimate cause which he calls God, and this
> access is infallible because it depends upon nothing
> but right thinking. In his thought he has not only con-
> trol over the idea of God, but also, in virtue of this, in
> the last resort, in the innermost depths of his spirit, he
> is identical with that ground of all things. That is the
> mystical or pantheistic foundation of every system. We
> say the same thing when we make the proposition that
> every system is a monologue of the thinker with him-
> self. Inasmuch as the world unfolds itself to him, it is
> his thinking self which unfolds itself therein. He puts
> the question, but it is he too who answers it to him-
> self.[47]

[47] Brunner, *God and Man*, 46-47.

Interestingly enough, in a polemical work against Barth and Brunner, a similar charge is made by Cornelius Van Til against "modern critical and idealistic speculation," but he includes Brunner's thought in this category and so concludes, "Brunner's divine-human encounter or correspondence turns out to be the speech that the modern autonomous man holds with himself."[48] In any event Van Til and Brunner are agreed that to adopt the presuppositions of critical metaphysics is to imply at the outset the identification, in principle, of the self with the whole nonhuman world.[49] They differ only in regard to the question whether Brunner and Barth have themselves adopted the critical presuppositions which imply a pantheistic standpoint.

3. *That Trust in Reason Implies Denial of the Paradoxical Christian Gospel.* The Kierkegaardians agree with Tertullian in his later years that from the standpoint of human reason the Christian gospel is impossible. Many foes of Christianity would heartily approve this sentiment. But to most Christian apologists it seems a strange phenomenon that defenders of the gospel should not only concede but insist upon the self-contradictory character of the Christian message. However, the irrationalists put forward several considerations to support this radical strategy.

First of all, they call the New Testament to witness. Jesus himself spoke in paradoxes. "He who finds his life will lose it, and he who loses his life for my sake will find

[48] *The New Modernism,* xvii-xviii.
[49] Cf. also Paul Lehmann, *Forgiveness,* 196-199.

it,"[50] he says, and again he prophesies that "many that are first will be last, and the last first."[51] In such declarations Jesus makes no effort to conform his statements to the requirements of reason, much less to establish them on rational grounds. Rather he appears to delight in confronting the wisdom of men with doctrines which seem to them impossible, but which are not so to God since "with God all things are possible."[52] The apostle Paul cries defiantly, "Jews demand signs and Greeks seek wisdom, but we preach Christ crucified, a stumbling-block to Jews and folly to Gentiles."[53] The paradox is to Paul not only doctrinal. It is also a matter of common experience in the Christian community.

> We are treated as impostors, and yet are true; as unknown, and yet well known; as dying, and behold we live; as punished, and yet not killed; as sorrowful, yet always rejoicing; as poor, yet making many rich; as having nothing, and yet possessing everything.[54]

The revelation of God is much better than all that human wisdom can discover. Hence "the desires of body and mind"[55] are linked together as belonging to the life of the unsaved. Salvation is not by these. Rather, he reminds the

[50] Matt. 10:39.
[51] Matt. 19:30.
[52] Matt. 19:26.
[53] I Cor. 1:22-23.
[54] II Cor. 6:8-10.
[55] Eph. 2:3.

Christians of Ephesus, they have had to be saved from them. It is "by grace you have been saved."[56]

Then, too, it is argued, the early Christians knew well that the gospel was an irresolvable paradox. It was not to be systematized but declared. They did not defend it by philosophical arguments but defended themselves by appeal to it as the word of God. The evidence for this contention is found both in the epistles of the New Testament and in the writings of the Church Fathers.[57] The approach which was made by the early Christian leaders to the world was such that it could not for a minute be confounded with the attempts of a philosopher to commend his system to critical readers. They simply declared the judgments of God which had been revealed to them. They did not call on men to judge them true or false. They acknowledged God as alone worthy to judge the truth of their testimony. Later, men became fearful and dubious about their gospel. Then they tried to bolster it up by the "evidences" dear to the philosopher. But in so doing they changed the whole character of their message from the revealed word of God to a human philosophy facing various philosophical rivals and seeking the approving judgments of human reason.

Finally, it is insisted, the character of the gospel itself shows its irrational nature. God and man are wholly other. What has He who was "in the beginning," before the earth or sun or stars—what has He in common with a hu-

[56] Eph. 2:5.
[57] Cf. pp. 37-43.

man being born only yesterday? Is the God who created all things like a man who cannot even add a cubit to his own stature? What similarity can be found between the God who alone is the holy Giver of the eternal law, the perfectly righteous, holy God and His weak, sinful subjects on earth? "His ways are not our ways." Yet the gospel is all based on God's having become man and having lived on earth as a helpless babe, a despised man, a man persecuted, spat upon and killed by other men. The eternal God crucified? The immortal Creator dying and laid in a sepulcher? Such is the old gospel story. Nor is it merely alleged that God *appeared* to be a man and *seemed* to die. That is not the gospel. Rather, say the revolters, He who would never deceive His children actually became man and truly died for their redemption. Self-contradictory? Absurd? Impossible? Of course. But nevertheless true. Small wonder, then, that when Kierkegaard would refer to the incarnation and crucifixion he often speaks simply of "the Paradox."[58]

So concludes the argument of the revolters. We may choose to be guided by reason in all things, even the quest for salvation and God. But by so doing, they insist, we shall be turning our backs on the Christian faith by which alone we might have been saved.

What can reason say in defense of itself?

[58] E.g., see *Fragments, passim.*

CHAPTER THREE

Reason's Defense

In examining the charges against reason, we shall of necessity appeal to reason. The investigation may therefore, at the outset, encounter an emphatic objection.

If the validity of reason is in question, how can we assume the competence of reason to determine the issue?

The reader may be reminded of a similar objection in the earlier arguments against Kierkegaard's own mode of attack. It will be remembered that when Kierkegaard used rational arguments against reason, it was objected by some of his critics that if he did not believe in reason he had no right to appeal to it for any purpose. In defense of Kierkegaard we said at that time that he did not regard reason as invalid for every task, but quite specifically for the tasks of inquiry concerning matters of infinite concern. Furthermore, it was observed that only by appealing to reason could he make an internal criticism of it such as would be admitted for consideration by rationalists themselves.

Similarly, when it is objected that Kierkegaard's charges should not be rationally evaluated, the objection must be

106

denied. Kierkegaard does not claim that reason is incompetent to observe its own limits. Rather, he emphatically asserts its usefulness to observe when its own bounds are passed.[1] Moreover, the revolters have chosen to carry the attack into the court of reason itself. If they had not done so, irrationalism in religion would have remained, as it had long been, a refuge of the ignorant. Its present vogue among intelligent and even learned people is due precisely to the intellectual respect afforded it by Kierkegaard's appeal to reason to rule against itself. The revolters cannot have their cake and eat it too. They cannot justly claim the right to enter the court of reason for the purpose of presenting evidence against the competence of the court and then at the same time deny the right of the court to hear arguments in its own defense.

What defense, then, may reason offer? At present we shall make the replies as strong as possible, leaving for the last chapter the task of measured evaluation.

A. REPLIES TO CHARGES AGAINST THE OBJECTIVE DETACHMENT OF REASON

1. The first charge which was brought against reason was that the cool, scientific impartiality which rational inquiry demanded was contrary to the commitments of a Christian. A Christian, it was said, has taken sides. To be impartial he would have to surrender his faith. He cannot, therefore,

[1] *Postscript*, 504.

make a cool, rational examination of his faith unless he first ceases to be a Christian. This charge the defenders of reason firmly deny.

The detachment which reason requires does not imply indifference. Rarely, if ever, is a mathematician or any other rational scholar really indifferent regarding the results of his more serious investigations. He is concerned with the discovery of something useful which will improve the conditions of life, or something new which will bring him fame, or at least something interesting which will bring him a kind of intellectual or aesthetic pleasure. Moreover, effective scientific inquiries are sometimes made into subjects with which the investigator has a deeply emotional concern. It was noted that a doctor usually prefers not to diagnose a serious illness of his wife or child. However, it occasionally becomes necessary that he do so, and in such instances a well-trained physician may be expected to do remarkably well. A scientific objectivity under such circumstances will require great effort, and it is natural that a man should desire to free himself from such an exacting and precarious undertaking. When it is not possible, a high degree of detachment can be obtained by means of a rigorous self-discipline. As the example suggests, rational objectivity is not a lack of concern but rather a disciplined control of emotional factors such as, to a greater or lesser degree, are almost invariably present.

Indeed, scientific impartiality is actually a product of passion. Such discipline as it requires cannot be achieved without intense motivation. Sometimes this motivation is provided by the sheer love of truth itself, sometimes by other interests, such as desire to cure the sick, to discover a military secret for winning a war, or to learn a moral truth by which a man may know and do his duty. Not infrequently a man's life depends on his ability to weigh objectively the factors in a situation involving acute danger. In the white heat of such passionate concern a man may achieve such a clear and balanced understanding of his circumstances and his powers as to arouse the amazement and admiration of everyone who has opportunity to contemplate his feat in retrospective leisure. Passion actually aids objectivity rather than interfering with it, provided the person who experiences it has learned to harness his deepest concerns to the burden of self-discipline.

Not only is rational detachment aided by some kinds of passionate interests; it is required by Christian love itself. "Thou shalt love the Lord thy God . . . with all thy mind." To love with the mind is to devote the mind at its best to the object of love. Certainly a mind which has forgotten its own essential loyalty to truth is not the mind at its best.

A Roman Catholic student once objected to the writer's exhortations to a spirit of disinterested inquiry in a class in philosophy. To weigh equitably considerations for and against such doctrines as the belief in God would be, she said, the vilest sin. She finally consented to continue the course, using the device of *imagining* what it *would* be like to consider freely the evidences for and against her most cherished beliefs. By the power of the imagination she was able to place herself outside the circle of her personal commitments and achieve a remarkable degree of intellectual detachment. Later she wrote that she would be forever grateful for having been led in this study to believe sincerely for the first time that God truly existed. Until then, she said, she had acted as if God existed, had faithfully repeated the creeds required of her and unhesitatingly told everyone that she believed in God. However, in her own heart of hearts she had always supposed that if she were ever to commit the "sin" of making a candid investigation, she would find that her belief was false. Now, she said, she was convinced, not only that it was required by her church and friends that she believe in God, but that in very truth God did exist. Was she not now able to love God with all her mind as never before?

2. But what shall we say to the charge that the mood of detachment required for the rational examination of basic religious doctrine is impossible? Are not such questions as concern the existence and love of God or one's own eternal salvation beyond the limits of any detached inquiry? How can any man be disinterested as he examines matters with which all of his interests are ultimately concerned? Can I be indifferent concerning the grounds of all the hope I have of lasting and supremely worthful life?

It may be conceded, at once, that in a matter of such profound concern as religious faith a perfect and permanent disinterestedness is impossible. At times, certainly, believer and unbeliever alike will be swayed by fear or hope, by sinful rebelliousness or by optimistic aspiration. But perfect and permanent detachment is not required, any more than an absolute, continuous pitch of passion is required to obey the injunction to love. A continuous mood of love may be possible, but no human being lives in the heat of a continuous single active affection. Nor is that required by the command to love. Similarly, all that is needed for the purpose of rational evaluation is an occasional assuming of the role of a disinterested spectator at times when evaluation of belief is being made.

The charge that objectivity is impossible overlooks the capacity of man to assume various roles alternately, in imagination. The power of imagination is actually part and parcel of the capacity to reason, as it is also of the capacity for sympathy and likewise for experiencing temptation. By imagination a disciplined mind can assume the role of spectator under any circumstances whatever, so long as the power of responsible choice remains at all. The brave and well-trained commander of a naval force, even while he is in the midst of a furious battle and in personal danger, can assume the role of a spectator to whom the units of the fighting fleets are pieces on a chessboard. He cannot be truly and constantly indifferent to the fact that one of these units is the flagship on which he stands. But he can act as if he were. He can plan the maneuvers of his fleet as if the safety of this ship were of no different concern to him than it would be to one of his observers high in the air above him.

Not only is it possible for a man to alternate in the roles of participant and critical spectator; it is even necessary that he do so if his own practical role in life is to be meaningful. I cannot know to my utmost ability what my own commitment means if I do not consider the meaning of alternative commitments of which my own implies the denial. If, on frequent occasions, I assume the role of detached spectator and critically relate the beliefs by which I live to all the evidence I have been able to find for and against them, my own life commitment will be deepened and broadened in meaning.[2]

3. The revolters have argued persuasively that much can be known by a person deeply involved in emotional commitments, which could not be learned by a person without such emotional experiences. In this stand they are undoubtedly right. Does it follow that the use of impartial reason results in the loss of truth? Not at all.

A detached inquirer is not a bloodless creature living in abstraction from life's emotional involvements. He is a human being with such loves and fears as all men experience. In his hours of deliberate, imaginative, self-disciplined detachment, he can and should include, among the evidences which he considers, the experiences of his most passionate involvements. If the data presented to a man of faith actually contradicted his commitment to the truth

[2] Cf. W. E. Hocking's doctrine of alternation in *The Meaning of God in Human Experience*.

itself, it would indeed be impossible to be loyal at once to truth and to such data. But surely the revolters do not believe that the experiences of faith are utterly illusory, nor that the belief in God, which faith affirms, is false. The more firmly one is convinced that the Christian faith is true, the more eager one should be to provide himself and others with proof of that fact by disinterested examination of the evidences for his faith in hours of disciplined detachment. What is needed would seem to be not a life of passionate disregard of truth on the one hand and a passionless indifference on the other, but a passionate search for the truth in which emotional experience will provide its full share of the evidence.

B. REPLY TO CHARGE AGAINST THE PRESUMPTION OF REASON

The revolters against reason have asserted that rational method implies the creation of idols. When human reason conceives of the deity to be worshiped and rules that the evidence is favorable to the worshiping of such a deity, man is creating his own God, it is said. Hence, the revolters conclude, rational method used in theology implies idolatrous faith.

Against the charge of idolatry the rational believer in God must enter earnest protest. Man is, to be sure, face to face with a real existential egocentric predicament. He must believe in the efficacy of something in himself if he is to be saved at all, whether by action, passion or reason. Minimizing reason and stressing passion in no way avoids that necessity.

But such belief in the human self does not imply idolatry. Reason may properly be regarded as God-given. Hence the use of reason may be gratefully regarded as the employment of a divine instrument. Furthermore, any rational believer in God will certainly regard human reason as incomparably inferior to divine reason. If I were able to use the reason of God instead of my own in the making of important decisions, I should certainly be irrational, as well as vain, not to do so. But for better or worse the reason which God has given and which He illuminates according to His own good pleasure is all that I have with which to know. The part of humility would seem to be, therefore, not the deprecating of this gift which God has benevolently provided, but rather the purifying of it by prayer and disciplined exercise, in order best to know the truth which is its proper object.

But Kierkegaard pointed out that when a man who believes in reason becomes convinced that his reason opposes faith in God, he then forsakes that faith. Therefore, the critical Dane argued, this man's real God is plainly not the one to whom he gives the name of deity, but rather his own reason, which he finally obeys. In reply it must be pointed out that when a man turns from a God who, he believes, does not actually exist, he does so in an earnest effort to *avoid* idolatry. To worship a nonexistent God would obviously be to worship a figment of man's own imagination. That would be idolatry indeed.

Such idolatry is, in fact, often practiced. Many millions of men have devoted themselves with passionate completeness to the worship of such fiendish deities as never existed save in the imagination. There has been no lack of existential faith in them. In obedience to their supposed commands thousands have fasted, burned themselves, cast themselves from precipices, endured shame, fought fanatically, and offered their own children as bloody sacrifices. Will we condemn the use of reason by which great multitudes have learned that such gods did not exist, and hence have been freed from their tyranny?

So long as one describes the truth of reason on the one hand, and God on the other, as alternatives between which a man must choose, we are at an impasse. But such a sad state of affairs is due to a quite gratuitous assumption. It would seem that the absolutely committed believer in God ought to be the last man to suggest that the reason which God has given to man has been thus incurably alienated from its proper object.

The vain and idolatrous pride of which rational believers are so often accused may at times be present, but reason has a cure for it. Will not reason teach man humility before his Maker? Will not reason instruct man to submit all his own opinions and desires to the bar of God's judgment? Is it not the very purpose of reason to provide a continuing criticism of our own vain desires and unsupportable opinions? When we deny the validity of reason as instrument of religious knowledge, we then open the door wide to a species of vanity which holds itself immune to all criticism. Certainly pride is not unknown among religious irrational-ists.[3] The real issue between humility and pride does not concern the question whether a man thinks himself greater or less than God. No man in his senses, who believes in God at all, dreams of equating himself with his Creator. The real issue concerns the relations between a man and his fellows. The believer in reason is required by his own principles to subject himself to the bar of candid criticism. This fact operates as a continual check on the universally human temptation to extravagant overappraisal of one's own opinions and actions. Once the arbitrament of reason is rejected, however, a man may be continually tempted to identify his own opinions with the thoughts of God Him-self and to repudiate the contrary ideas of his fellows as the wily devices of Satan. Whatever his convictions about the necessity of submitting his own thoughts to the judgments of God, in the practical problems of his human social con-text the judgments of God may be difficult to identify. He and his fellows may find no norm but reason to which they can make common appeal for the arbitration of their differ-ences.

[3] Cf. Dean Willard L. Sperry's remarks on the humility and pride of liberals and their critics in *Religion and Life*, XVI, No. 3 (Summer, 1947), 334-335. Cf. also Kierkegaard's belief that his martyrdom was due to his being "a genius living in a market town" (see p. 51, n. 52). More reliance on reason could have provided him with a cure for such lofty condescension toward his fellow citizens in Copenhagen.

That the advantages of rationalism as a means of promoting humility are not purely theoretical may be negatively evidenced by observing both the tone and the method of such a work as the "Angry Introduction" and the succeeding pages of Karl Barth's polemic against Emil Brunner entitled *No!* Bearing in mind the long and intimate association of these two men in the development and promotion of the "Dialectical Theology" and the continued expressions of appreciation and friendship by Brunner, the reader finds Barth writing such passages as the following:

> If this is Brunner's opinion—and how can I, how can anyone, doubt any longer that this is indeed the case?—then I fail to understand among many other things the following: how can he think that, in spite of this opinion, he has a right to be mentioned "in one breath" with—of all people—me, to be my "ally," my "good friend," and that I have merely failed to understand him and therefore have in error shot at him by night? . . .
>
> Brunner does not understand or will not understand, or does not wish to show and to say that he understands, that the issue between himself and myself is such that to-day it can only be decided openly and consciously. . . .
>
> But it should not be held against me if in these pages I appear in a thoroughly exclusive and unfriendly attitude; if the reader now sees an unedifying disruption where before he thought to see unity; and

if my answer lacks that "elegance" for which Brunner's essay is praised. At the moment I am not worried about elegance.[4]

When a person accustomed to the self-critical, co-operative methods of truth-seeking among scientists and philosophers reads through Barth's pages of violent denunciation, invective and unsupported assertions, he is bound to ask, Is this the humility for which I am asked to give up the "pride of reason"? Remembering the persistent self-criticism and calls to others for help from an Isaac Newton or Marie Curie, a Plato or Alfred North Whitehead, he may add that reason has its humility which the dogmatists know not of. To be sure, there have been arrogant assertions and denunciations by distinguished users of reason too. But it is obvious that in such utterances they were not appealing to reason. Their pride appeared when they neglected reason, not when they depended upon it.

C. REPLIES TO CHARGES THAT REASON IS INEFFECTIVE

A third type of charge against reason is that it is ineffective as a means of reaching the kind of truth demanded by the interests of religious faith. While not claiming that human reason is a perfect instrument, nor even that it approaches perfection, its defenders reject the specific charges made

[4] From Peter Fraenkel's translation of Barth, *No!* which appears together with Brunner, *Nature and Grace* in a single volume entitled *Natural Theology*, 70-73.

against it on the ground of its ineffectiveness. The replies to these charges will be taken up in order.

1. Kierkegaard has made much of the fact that rational method cannot attain absolute certainty, while he has pointed out the need for such certainty when an individual's eternal destiny is at stake.

It must be freely admitted that absolute certainty, regarding most matters of importance at least, is beyond the reach of human reason. It should be added that it is beyond the reach of man, whatever instrument he may choose for its attainment. In practice we have not the choice between absolute certainty and none. We do, however, have the choice between more certainty and less. Surely some beliefs are more probable than are others. Is it not right that we should prefer the more probable to the less probable? Is there any self-contradiction involved in the persevering effort of a rationalist to discover ever more and yet more probability? Sometimes the evidence may even become so overwhelming that within the context of limited human knowledge the probability may without impropriety be called certainty, or at least relative certainty. This is the proper object of rational search and not that unattainable abstraction, apodictic certainty.

If a higher degree of probability is better than a lower degree, there is much to be said in favor of critical rational inquiry. Without such investigation a man may affirm his belief with every kind of emotional assertiveness. Violent affirmation may in some quarters be accounted as certainty.

But a more meaningful and sincere assurance has been attained by many a thinker who has calmly weighed all the evidence which he could discover, both for and against his faith, and has come to a serene and clear conviction of its truth.

2. The revolters have objected that if reason could attain certainty faith would be destroyed. Faith, they insist, is a kind of passion and passion cannot be induced except in a condition of tension. The serenity of rational certainty would be an absence of tension and hence a condition in which faith could not occur.

In reply, it must be admitted that there is a kind of excitement possible in a condition of emotional conflict which is impossible without it. If a man makes a life commitment contrary to his own reason, he will experience a kind of agitation which will not be present in the experience of a man whose reason and will are in serene harmony. It may be suspected that the popularity now enjoyed by paradoxical writings in theology is in part due to the excitement which they induce in the reader.

However, the tensions of life which are capable of arousing the will to wholehearted action will not be for long relieved in this life. The world is filled with sin. The prevalence of fear, hate, destruction and hunger should provide any person of good will with quite sufficient tension to stir his best mettle. Surely there is no sign that any Christian will soon contemplate a world in which there is no work to be done. If the believer's reason supports his faith, then he can devote his full energies to fighting against war, unfair racial and class discrimination, impurity, rampant selfishness, and all other expressions of atheism in the world. There is a kind of person who much prefers to fight his battles within himself, setting his will against his reason, for example. Such a person may by the internal friction of his own soul use up all the energies which he is capable of generating, with not an ounce to spare for pulling a load. But is not such a personal condition pitiable? Is it not better to work for such complete integration of reason and passion within that the full powers of the soul may be brought to bear on the evils of a sinful world?

The stress of the revolters on the value of tension does have one value. It is to be hoped that it will serve as a counterbalance to an opposite trend of recent preaching. Of late many ministers have falsely identified Christian salvation with the psychologist's ideal of personal integration. The Scriptures, history and the contemporary scene all give abundant evidence that the agonized soul is often much more useful to the world and also much nearer Christ than the most contented representative of serene sanity. Mere freedom from spiritual conflict is one of the most wretched ideals ever to lull a congregation into complacency.

What is needed, however, is neither tension per se nor freedom from tension, but an earnest desire to know and do the will of God. If a person genuinely seeks first the kingdom of God, he will find plenty of tension between himself and the world to demand the most valiant faith and passionate devotion.

3. Kierkegaard and his disciples deny that doubt may be cured by reason. Doubt, they argue, is not caused by reason but by sin. Consequently it cannot be removed by reason, but only by repentance at the Cross.

Some doubt does, assuredly, result from sinful rebellion. Every teacher and minister has observed instances of persons who, desiring to evade their religious duties, have conjured up a succession of doubts to afford them escape. Every doubt answered for such an individual is merely the occasion for generating some new objection to the religious belief which would imply the necessity of sacrifice and toil.

The apologist of faith must, however, beware of impugning the motives of all who disbelieve. Unbelievers as well as believers can cry "rationalization!" Not only does some belief in God result psychologically from wishful thinking, but sometimes it is actually a sinful projection of selfishness. Religion does serve for some persons as an opiate, enabling them to enjoy positions of privilege and luxury in the midst of want, on the supposition that God willed it so and intends in his own good time to reward all who now must suffer.

Charges of wishful thinking against believers and unbelievers alike make for little advance toward truth. This fact is recognized by great numbers of earnest but intelligent persons who are determined to avoid a mere projecting of their desires and fears, and rather to discover what is really so. Great numbers of such seekers after truth are beset by doubts that are utterly sincere. Evidence of that sincerity is found in the fact that many young people in college who have learned to doubt and to leave the faith of their parents have returned to glowing faith and loyal service when they have been convinced by rational evidence that their doubts were unfounded.

Doubts which are the mere projection of emotion must admittedly be met by an indirect approach. On the other hand, doubts which are rationally produced must be dealt with rationally. As Duvall has written, "The awakened mind finds that wounds struck by reason can be healed by reason alone."[5] Many a college youth has had his faith done irreparable damage when his spiritual advisers have refused to deal rationally with the first questionings of his reason. Such treatment has only convinced him that the doubts were well founded and the doctrines he has been asked to affirm untrue.

Even when doubt has been caused by emotional projection, rational treatment may well serve as a part of the total program of diagnosis and cure. In most cases it is difficult to know whether unbelief is a mere rationalization or a quite sincere result of earnest thought, until a rational approach has been tried. Such an approach, however, will sometimes jolt the doubter into a recognition of the deeper volitional sources of his questionings.

No intelligent person would argue that dispassionate

[5] Trumbull G. Duvall, *Great Thinkers*, 15.

reason was the only method which ought to be used in the treatment of doubt, whether the unbelief concerned the existence of God or the fidelity of the doubter's wife. But to omit the use of reason altogether would seem even less defensible than to place sole reliance upon it.

4. Kierkegaard has maintained that reason continually seeks to know existence but that in order to do so it must commit suicide. For reason, he holds, knows only concepts and never comprehends existing particulars.

This is a strange teaching. Reason, we have noted, is simply a person thinking. To maintain that no person ever knows any existing thing as existing is, indeed, hard doctrine. To be sure, without a concept reason cannot operate. Moreover, it is always possible to raise a question whether any concept truly represents any particular thing. But all thinking, including all of Kierkegaard's, is based on the assumption that some concepts do represent existing realities. What must be affirmed here is simply that every act of knowledge about existence is at the same time an act of faith. It is always possible to argue that the ideas I have of other persons, of things, and even of myself, may be groundless dreams, but by faith I know that it is not so.

More than once, in their discussions of this problem, the revolters seem to confuse knowledge by acquaintance and knowledge about it. The English language is peculiarly deficient in its use of the same word "know" to mean both. It is one thing to know who Mr. Jones is. It is another thing to know him. The two kinds of epistemological relation supplement and enrich each other, but they should not be confused. If I am to know God as I long to know Him, I must meet Him in divine-human encounter such as Brunner has so persuasively described. But if I am to know Him as I long to know Him, I must also have some true ideas about Him.

The relationship of man to God is by no means devoid of all mediation by universals. He can in truth confront me directly in the privacy and particularity of my own soul. But when He does so I recognize Him as the One about whom I have heard and thought in various terms. He is, for example, the Creator, Judge, Redeemer and Father of Whom I have read in the Scriptures.

It may be freely admitted that concepts and moral laws, in themselves, have no power to save. But they are highly useful as the schoolmaster introducing us into the very presence of Him who can save. The God who saves us is not an impetuous and arbitrary master. He does, in truth, demand that we give ourselves, soul and body, to Him. But this which he demands is a "reasonable service."[6] It is because of the harmony and meaningfulness of this service that we rightly love and revere Him, as well as fear Him.

[6] Romans 12:1. Here the familiar version of 1611 is quoted in preference to the Revised Standard Version employed elsewhere. The author sees no objection to the revisers' substitution of "worship" for "service" in this passage, but can find no reason to substitute "spiritual" for "reasonable" as the translation of a Greek adjective which is the etymological equivalent of the English word "logical" and which is usually understood to mean rational, intellectual or sensible.

5. The irrationalists tell us that God is so completely different from man that human reason is utterly incapable of discovering Him. All reason, they say, proceeds from the known to the unknown, using similarities as bridges for its passage. But between man and God there are no similarities. He is the Wholly Other. The chasm between ourselves and Him cannot possibly be bridged by reason.

It may be freely admitted that God is Wholly Other in the sense of a complete nonidentity. Man is not God nor any aspect nor part of Him. There is no element of being which is both in God and in man. His being and ours do not overlap at any point. In that sense we may truly say that God has nothing in common with us. However, it is quite another thing to say that He is in no way *similar* to us. The Kierkegaardians would surely have to admit that they themselves believe God to be real and likewise apply the notion of reality to man. To be sure, God's reality is absolute and unconditioned whereas ours is a conditioned reality. But reality as such is truly attributed both to God and to man, nevertheless. Furthermore, nothing is clearer than that the New Testament attributes the same kind of love both to God and to man. "We love, because he first loved us."[7] Surely love is no trivial experience. If we are capable, by God's grace, of experiencing the kind of love which He also experiences, then we have something exceedingly important in common with Him. Moreover, even those relations in which we are most obviously different

[7] I John 4:19.

from God are shared relations. Both God and man have participated in creation: God by creating, man by being created. Both God and man are involved in redemption: God by redeeming, man by being redeemed. Even such relations may well serve as bridges over which reason can pass. That creation has actually served in this way will be immediately recognized by anyone who recalls the cosmological and teleological arguments.

Kierkegaard makes much of what he calls the absolute "Paradox," the incarnation. But if, as Kierkegaard insists, God did actually become man and die as man, then it is clear that, despite the Dane's contrary assertion, divinity and humanity do have something in common. Even if such incarnation seems impossible to us, the fact of its having occurred, if such be the fact, would prove that it is not impossible to God. If there were absolutely nothing analogous in the life of man and the life of God, then for God to become man would be not only a miracle passing all bounds of understanding; it would be an utterly meaningless miracle. Whatever happened in the actual life and death of Jesus, the history of theology and the life of the world in subsequent centuries have certainly proved that it was not meaningless.

There is something quite absurd in the irrationalists' insisting that no human knowledge of God is possible, while at the same time they continue to describe Him in various conceptual terms. They do this every time they say a word about Him. Of course, no man has found God by his own powers alone. No man even exists by his own powers alone. While existing, no man knows any other being by his own powers alone. Man does not live alone. From birth until death he is in meaningful interaction with the creative activity of God and the activities of other persons. But with the help of God many men do come to know Him, in however fragmentary a fashion.

If it is replied that the knowledge of God which is attained by some men is not the product of reason but rather of God's revelation, it must be replied that reason never works alone. It is the very nature of reason to employ all the data which experience can provide. If at times God penetrates the experience of man with His own revealing presence, such significant experience must surely be included by reason in its truth-seeking work. By whatever means God is known, the revolters would be among the first to insist that they do know Him. Either they know Him as truly real or they think of Him as merely an imaginary construction. If the latter is the case then faith is false; if the former, then the irrationalists themselves know God as truth. Since reason is simply the person thinking in quest of truth, reason has, by the revolters' testimony, attained the object which they have objected it would never reach. That the initiative of God has played an indispensable part in the process, and that apart from Him man's reason would not even exist, let alone know any object, is readily agreed by the theistic rationalist.

6. One of the objections to reason in religion is that such evil as that now experienced by millions of people is

not capable of any reasonable account. We have noticed that this objection has seemed especially overwhelming to many Europeans. Reason, they say, must insist that a good God would not permit such awful tragedy. Yet the tragedy is here. Therefore, either a good God does not exist or reason is unreliable. They choose the latter horn of the dilemma.

Reason must reply that if its own norms are to be obeyed, no decision may be based upon the data of one continent, nor even the experience of the whole world in one generation alone, when more data are available. It is true, of course, that for a prosperous American to evaluate the eternal purposes of God by reference only to the pleasant state of his own existence would be quite unreasonable. On the other hand, it is just as contrary to reason to base our cosmic view upon the worst experience of an especially tragic generation. Reason demands wholeness and must therefore insist upon the most comprehensive view of the world which can be attained by any means whatsoever.

One kind of evil we may promptly admit is irrational. It is of the very nature of sin to be contrary to reason. But sin would not have the meaning of sin at all were it not a revolt within the universal context of an essentially rational order. The fact of sin emphasizes the capacity of man himself for rationality. It even underlies his intuition that the rational alone is normative. It is because man can be rational and knows that he ought to be, that he cannot come to terms with his own irrational choices.

Natural evil is far from being completely explained in

detail. On the other hand, we are just as far from a demonstration that it is in principle unexplainable. What should be believed about its origin and its relation to reasonable and righteous purpose can only be learned, if at all, by rational inquiry, making use of all the data available, including, of course, such experiences as may be regarded as divine revelations.

If "reality itself is a system for God" as Kierkegaard says,[8] then while granting that it "cannot be a system," perfect and absolute, for a created "existing spirit," we may yet believe that such a person may approach, by His help, more and more nearly to God's own systematic view of the world. Since by Kierkegaard's own testimony reality is "a system for God," no unsystematic view can be true. When the revolters profess that God has revealed to them that existence is "unsystematic" and even self-contradictory, while God Himself holds a systematic view, they make of Him a great deceiver.

D. REPLIES TO CHARGES OF EVIL RESULTS

1. The revolters are in error when they argue that the pursuit of philosophy prevents a man from making decisions. Actually no human philosopher is a disembodied passive speculator. He must of necessity live in commitment to some principles. They may be principles which he has objectively examined in his philosophy, or they may be

[8] *Postscript*, 107.

as completely uncritical as those of a man who does not believe in philosophy at all; but every human being, philosopher or not, makes decisions and commits himself to one way of life or another. There need be no fear, then, that the pursuit of philosophy will keep a man from making some decisions, though, like many an unphilosophical person, the thinker may make the wrong decisions or be cowardly in the sustaining of his own choices.

Moreover, reason actually commands practical absolutism. A philosopher who is determined to act in accordance with reason should know that he cannot possibly make his life count heavily for truth by means of tentative or half-hearted commitment. To be sure, even if he devotes himself with utmost zeal to the principles which seem to him on the whole most reasonable, he may miss the truth. But if he fails to devote himself wholeheartedly to the support of any principle, he is sure to miss the truth. If he be a true lover of rational wisdom, therefore, he will be bound to observe the necessity of thoroughgoing personal commitment.

2. It has been argued by Emil Brunner and others that the belief in rational method as an instrument for knowing God will lead any thinker who is consistent to a pantheistic view of God's relations to the world. It will be remembered that this argument was to the effect that if God is to be known by human reason, it must be because human reason and God have something in common. If they have some-

thing in common, then God overlaps man, which is to say that man is a part of God.

This argument is inaccurate, for actually reason may be thoroughly believed in as an instrument for knowing God without implying that any part of God is identical with any part of man. All that is required by reason is that there be some relations between God and man. There must be in human experience some elements which are at least similar to elements in the being or activity of God. But similarity is not identity and relatedness need not imply overlapping. To believe that by reason we may know God does imply that the world is a system and not a chaos of unrelated elements. But even Kierkegaard believes that the world is known to God as a system, which is to say that in truth it is a system. Reason requires no more to give it an open avenue from creature to creator.

The objection to reason which we are discussing might equally well be employed to support the view that no man could know his brother without being his brother or being some part of him. Actually the knowledge of one man by another is a common enough experience, and much of such knowledge is obviously rational. So long as a man has some relations with his brother, whether of conversation, or co-operation, or even conflict, he has the means which reason requires for achieving knowledge of his brother.

The revolters seem to assume that all rational knowledge is of the kind described by epistemological monists. It is difficult to embrace the view that in knowledge idea and object are identical without implying that knowledge of

God would be impossible unless at some point, at least, God and the knowing man are identical. However, it is well known that comparatively few thinkers in the history of philosophy have believed that idea and object are necessarily identical in rational knowledge. Many philosophers believe that an idea is never identical with the object which it knows. In any event, the strongest reply which can be made by the rationalist to the charge of implying pantheism is a vigorous assertion of the view known among philosophers as epistemological dualism. When I know my friend, or a star, or God, I do not assert by my knowledge that any idea of mine is my friend, or the star, or God, or any part of these objects.

Actually, if the revolters are anxious to dispose of pantheism they will do well to leave off their hostility to reason and to call upon the rationalist for help. The principal objections to pantheism are rational objections. The assertion that God is all that is, implies the denial of genuine error and minimizes the seriousness of sin. In view of the fact that both error and sin are frequently experienced by us all, it is highly irrational to embrace pantheism. The belief in reason, so far from implying pantheism implies the denial of it.

3. The revolters have argued that the New Testament and the Church Fathers are irrationalistic and that the gospel is fundamentally paradoxical. However, these objections appear to be based on misunderstanding or exaggeration.

The New Testament employs reason with utmost freedom. Jesus used arguments from analogy,[9] pragmatic arguments,[10] and arguments a fortiori.[11] He argues frequently from cause to effect and appeals again and again to experience for the correction of notions which he regards as theologically or ethically mistaken.[12] St. Paul, whom the revolters are especially fond of quoting in their belief, is described in the Acts as entering into argumentative discussion in place after place which he visited for missionary purposes.[13] Much of the New Testament is written in the spirit of Isaiah's words, " 'Come now, and let us reason together,' saith Jehovah."[14] When we are exhorted to commit ourselves wholly to God it is added "which is your reasonable service."[15] The appeals to reason in the Fourth Gospel are widely known. From the prologue, based upon a revision of the prevailing Logos philosophy, to the promise of Christ, "You will know the truth and the truth will make you free,"[16] the Fourth Gospel is a highly rational, as well as mystical document. Even when Jesus and St. Paul used the paradox as a rhetorical device, it seems often to have been an intentional means of stimulating more earnest and penetrating thought. "For whoever would save

[9] E.g., Matt. 5:43-45; 6:30; Luke 15.

[10] See especially Matt. 7:15-20; Luke 7:20-23; 13:6-9.

[11] E.g., Matt. 7:11 and Luke 13:15-17.

[12] E.g., Matt. 5:46-47, but especially Luke 13:1-5.

[13] Note the many occurrences of the word διαλέγομαι (discuss, dispute, reason with) in the accounts of Paul's missionary labors.

[14] Isa. 1:18. In quotations from the Old Testament the American Standard Revised Version has been followed.

[15] Rom. 12:1.

[16] John 8:32.

his life will lose it"[17] implies no logical contradiction, since
the saving and losing have obviously to do with different
levels of being. But the utterance of such a paradox does
tend to set the hearer to thinking about his experience, and
by the rational contemplation of such experiences as Jesus'
words recall to mind, he may well come to a profounder
understanding of his duty, which is to say, of God's will
for him.

When we turn from the New Testament to the Church
Fathers, we do find, without doubt, some men deeply dis-
trustful of reason. Even a Tertullian or a Tatian, however,
while often expressing distrust of reason, will be found to
appeal to it on innumerable occasions, in support of his
theological positions. It is noteworthy, also, that in some
instances, as in the life of Tertullian, the more extreme
irrationalism occurred precisely at that period in his life
when he was drifting away from the great central doctrines
of the Christian Church and embracing positions later
recognized by all classes of Christians as heretical. On the
other hand, surely no one can doubt that a number of the
Church Fathers were among the most rationalistic thinkers
the Church has ever produced. Justin Martyr, for example,
after being trained in Greek philosophy, carried over into
his Christian ministry the dialectical skills which he had
learned. Indeed one authority tells us that the custom of
wearing robes in the pulpit originated in Justin's use of the

[17] Mark 8:35.

philosopher's robe during his own preaching.[18] Consistently enough, he maintained that if he had a right to wear a robe of wisdom before his conversion, he had a greater right after it, for his Christian wisdom was greater than any he had possessed before. Clement of Alexandria is another great thinker of the Early Church whose rationalism no one could doubt. He says in so many words, "Everything that is contrary to right reason is sin."[19] Many of the early apologists not only appealed to reason in defense of their theology, but even quoted with approval passage after passage from the pagan philosophers themselves to demonstrate the reasonableness of the gospel.

Undoubtedly there is a sense in which the gospel is paradoxical. It is wonderful. It passes the bounds of our experience and understanding that there should exist a Being able to create us and the world in which we live. It is even more wonderful that such a Creator should love us and tenderly care for us, even suffer for us, while we are in sinful rebellion against Him. Yet there is nothing in the gospel which contradicts the principles of reason nor the data of our experience. The argument that Christian teaching is essentially paradoxical, that is, self-contradictory, assumes gratu-

[18] Alexander Roberts and James Donaldson, *The Ante-Nicene Fathers,* Vol. I, 160. Cf. the footnote on the same page concerning the philosopher's gown: "It survives in the pulpits of Christendom—Greek, Latin, Anglican, Lutheran, etc.—to this day, in slightly different forms."

[19] *The Instructor* I, 13. Cf. his definition, "And Christian conduct is the operation of the rational soul in accordance with a correct judgment and aspiration after the truth, which attains its destined end through the body, the soul's consort and ally." *Ibid.*

itously some irrational doctrines. If, for example, it is maintained that the infinite God who is absolutely other than man became man while He continued to be absolutely other than man, one has indeed asserted self-contradiction. In so far as he has done so, he has simply erased the meanings of his own words and left letters upon the page or sounds in the air, which, however well calculated to stir pious sentiment in some hearers, convey no intelligible meaning. But the doctrine that God is in no way similar to man, and that, while being utterly dissimilar He yet was man, is to be found nowhere in the New Testament. For such contradictions in thought we should not hold the gospel writers responsible, but rather the speculative theologians of later centuries who proceeded with greater respect for cumulative traditions and the practical needs of propaganda against despised heresies than for critical self-restraint. Kierkegaard tells us that for God all is systematic. If the gospel be true, then the gospel is not paradoxical to Him. If it is not paradoxical to God, then in truth it is not so. Herein is ground of hope that with sufficiently critical use of the reason which God has given us and with growing experience of His grace we may progressively surmount the seeming contradictions which have puzzled the minds of inquirers through centuries past.

CHAPTER FOUR

Objections to Irrationalism

We have been considering some of the replies which may well be made in refutation of the charges against rational methods in theology. Believers in the use of reason are not content, however, with defense. They seek not only to refute the objections made by the revolters against reason, but also to point out the weaknesses in the position of the irrationalists themselves. Some of the chief objections to irrationalism will now be brought forward.

1. Irrationalism Is Self-destructive. Either an irrationalist will try to maintain his irrationalism consistently or he will not. If he does not try to do so he is obviously half-hearted in his revolt against reason. A man who writes articles and books denouncing reason as instrument of religious knowledge and announcing the superiority of the paradox in theology can hardly ask to be taken seriously if he does not try to make his own detailed beliefs and his doctrinal preaching conform to his avowed principle. For then he will be denying in his concrete theological pronouncements that very irrationalism the denial of which he denounces in other theologians. If he does not mean to practice in his teaching about God, his christology, or his doctrine of salvation what he preaches about the futility of reason in theology, then he had better leave off his preaching of irrationalism to other people until he has persuaded himself.

But suppose he does try to bring all his doctrinal preaching into conformity with his profession of irrationalism. He will then be paying solemn tribute to the very principle which he most despises. Every paradox he utters and every mystery with which he bewilders his reader will doubtless be put forth with the satisfaction of a man of principle, steering a course consistent with his avowed ideals. But alas! one implication of *his* ideal is that a man must not care about consistency. He has insisted that principles cannot serve as guides in particular choices. He has repudiated the concern with consistency as the self-worship of human reason. Now he finds that the effort to be faithful to his irrationalism involves him in the "idolatry" he sought to renounce forever.

The revolter is in a dilemma, indeed. Shall he try to be true to his revolutionary profession or not? At every moment when he willingly deviates from it, preferring to abide by the norms of reason in preference to mystery and insoluble paradox, he pays willing tribute to reason and denies his profession. But at every moment when he wills to be faithful to his principle, rejecting logical norms and preferring his paradoxes instead, he is willingly, even with stern determination, paying tribute to that very norm which he despises most of all, the norm of logical consistency as guide in religious thought. Ironically, the rebels who would deny the validity of reason as arbiter in theology are doomed to spend their lives paying voluntary theological tribute to that selfsame reason.

In practice, the revolters appear to sense these self-destructive implications of their own irrationalism, and hence to seek vainly some way of evading them. They seem never to have made up their minds whether it is better to hold steadfastly to their espoused view or not. Now they glory in the contradictory character of their doctrines, for example, concerning necessity and responsibility, as exemplifying the paradoxical nature of truth. But now again they scorn the positions of their opponents, whether in their own camp or outside, because of their real or fancied illogical character. They insist, in rational fidelity to their principle, that all human argumentation about God and salvation is futile. But they are the most incessant debaters of the age. So they swing back and forth from the one testimony to the validity of reason to the other, trying constantly but in vain to escape what might well be called, in the words of Hegel, "the guile of reason."

The net effect of all this is not to overthrow reason, but merely to muddy the waters of thought. Theological dilettantism is supported and men who are so inclined are given encouragement to substitute unsupported assertion or denunciation for measured thought.

2. *The Paradox as Used by the Revolters Threatens the Very Possibility of Communication.* All communication between one human being and another depends upon a certain stability of ideas. When a man tells me that he is a Republican, but of course he is a Democrat, I may understand him to be telling me in facetious fashion that he, like other members of the Republican party, believes in many democratic principles; but if he tells me that he is at one and the same time completely loyal to both of two opposing political parties, he leaves me quite unenlightened regarding his position. His talk has been only sound and fury signifying nothing. Communication has broken down.

The paradox is an ancient device highly useful for gaining attention and making men think about neglected aspects of their experience. But the paradox is useful for communication only so far as it arouses the reason of the hearer to harmonize the seeming contradictions. When Heraclitus says that the "way up and the way down are the same," his effort at communication fails completely unless the reader thinks sufficiently patiently and penetratingly to understand that, regardless of the question whether matter is being transformed from earth to fire or from fire to earth, an orderly change is taking place, and that Heraclitus is insisting that change and its laws alone truly exist. When Socrates declares that he is the wisest man in Athens because he knows that he knows nothing, communication fails unless his hearers go on to reason that Socrates is not really contradicting himself but only giving them a new insight into a love of wisdom and a critical method which count the little knowledge already gained as but loss, as compared with the vast realm of indefiniteness and mystery which yet remains. Paradoxes, in short, are useful so long as we look for the truth, not in them, but in a new rational synthesis beyond them. This does not appear to be the intention of Kierkegaard nor of the men most influenced by him.

3. *The Internal Meaning of a System of Belief Concerning Existence Cannot Be Maintained Independent of All Rational Grounds.* When the rationalists are insisting that only consistency can give to attempts at communication any intelligible meaning, the revolter may reply that the meaning of his doctrine may be maintained by internal consistency while the grounds of his position are completely independent of reason. Actually, all words which have to do with existence at all take their meaning either directly or indirectly from experience. The positivists who maintain that all meaning must be derived from sense experience are undoubtedly mistaken. There are experiences of spirit as well as of matter, and such words as "love" and "thought" derive their primary meanings from such experiences. On the other hand, a word which made no reference, direct or

indirect, to any kind of experience whatsoever would surely be meaningless gibberish.

When, therefore, it is denied that belief in God is grounded in any experience, it is denied that such belief can have any meaning for man. If God is in no way analogous to man or to any other object of rational experience, then for man all meaning is removed from the word "God." If this were actually true, the use of the word would signify nothing, and any other combination of letters and sounds might as well be employed. In practice, however, the most ardent of the irrationalists in Christian theology do make many affirmations concerning God—affirmations which obviously derive their meanings by analogy from experiences of human personality and, by inference, from our knowledge of causal relations.

Much of the attractiveness of many writings by such men as Kierkegaard and Niebuhr is due precisely to the daring and dramatic analogies by means of which they give concrete meaning to their conceptions of God. The reader of the *Philosophical Fragments* is not likely soon to forget Kierkegaard's story of the masquerading royal suitor as a figure of the Incarnation. To be sure, no intelligent reader supposes that the author is giving a literal description of God. Indeed, Kierkegaard takes pains to point out some important differences between the king seeking to win the sincere love of a humble maiden and God seeking the love of a human sinner. For example, he says that the Incarnation is not a mere masquerade, for God is no deceiver and hence could not appear as man without in very truth becoming man. But no analogy can teach anything unless there is *some* real similitude. In this instance Kierkegaard's story is utterly pointless if God is not like the king at least in this, that He has a purpose and adopts a course designed to accomplish that purpose. It is obvious that the author actually believes there are other similarities, too. Both God and the king have purposes which require changes of heart in their subjects, and such changes of heart as can be brought about only by a self-abasement of the ruling sovereigns. Both, moreover, willingly make the necessary sacrifices, though God's is so much greater and so much purer in motive that they are hardly worthy to be compared. All the quantitative and qualitative differences cannot conceal the implicit teaching that the God represented here is not *wholly* other in kind but is in some ways strikingly similar to man.

Any such discovery of analogous relations between men and God is a quite rational procedure. At one and the same time it gives meaning to the affirmations concerning God and also plausibility. If all such rational grounds of theistic doctrine were to be eliminated from the writings of the revolters there would remain little to identify those writings as having anything to do with religion in general or Christian doctrine in particular.

4. Only by Much Rational Knowledge of God Could It Be Known That He Was of Such a Character as to Be beyond Rational Knowledge. It has often been pointed out by the critics of complete philosophical skepticism that to establish skepticism a man would need to be omniscient. How can a thinker know that nothing can ever be known, unless he knows so much about everything there is as to be sure that all is of such character as to be unknowable? Similarly, it is difficult to understand how anyone could possibly know that the character of God was beyond rational knowledge. To be sure, some being other than a human being might conceivably know that God was of such a nature as to be beyond human powers of knowledge. But the revolters are fond of reminding us that man must ever remember that it is only as man that he can hope to know God at all. As man he cannot relate the limitations of his reason to the reality, God, without this rational operation of relating actually bringing God into the circle of rational inquiry. Kierkegaard himself has told us that reason is useful in determining when its own bounds have been passed. But surely reason cannot observe any idea or experience which is beyond the bounds of its own observation. By the very act of observing that such an object was beyond the ken of reason it would have brought the supposedly unknowable experience within the circle of rational observation.

The revolters may try to escape this objection by replying that their knowledge of the God who is beyond reason comes to them not through reason but through revelation. But this is really beside the point. Let us suppose, for the

145

moment, that God has become known through some totally nonrational process of revelation. As soon as a theologian sought to judge whether such a God was beyond all rational knowledge he would have to reason about Him. Of course, in doing so he would of necessity represent Him by a rational concept. If, as Kierkegaard argues in the *Fragments*, no concept can make a valid representation of Him, then the concept by which the theologian now seeks to represent God fails in its function. Hence, the theologian is not actually demonstrating the absolute transcendence by a concept which by his own testimony misrepresents God. The man who seeks by thinking accurately to prove the impossibility of thinking accurately about God must begin by assuming the falsehood of the proposition he is trying to establish.

5. Reason Is Needed to Distinguish between True and False Revelations. If there is some revelation by which a man may know God, the validity of that revelation must somehow be distinguished from all the false claims of revelation. Moreover, since we are but men, and since we are called upon to live as men, we cannot avoid the necessity of making this distinction as men. As soon as we are seeking to find out what is the difference between the true revelation and its false competitors, we are employing human reason by the very definition of the revolters, for we are using the powers of men thinking in search for truth.

The fact that human reason must be employed to distinguish truly revealed doctrine from teaching which is falsely claimed to be revealed is acknowledged in striking fashion by the irrationalists. Of course, they do not say in so many words that they must depend upon reason for any such task, nor do they admit that they would encourage others to do so. Yet by their actions they pay constant tribute to reason as the instrument to be employed for this very purpose.

Where, among all the theologians and philosophers of the twentieth century, can one find more incessant debaters than among the revolters against reason? Everywhere, from printing presses, pulpits, classroom desks and forum plat-forms, come their continual arguments. They never stop telling the world the superior merits of the particular chan-nels of revelation in which they believe as compared with all others. They do this by insisting upon the inconsisten-cies, superficialities, infidelities to experience, and subtle self-deceptions present in rival systems of doctrine.

What could be more rational than such critical method-ology? Yet when the same critical instruments are turned upon their own ideas, they perpetually cry, "Of course, we know that we are inconsistent, but the truth is paradoxical and so must we be if we are to be right."

The reader is reminded of Tertullian, who warned the defenders of the Rule of Faith that they ought not to argue with heretics by appeal to the Scriptures "on points in which victory will either be impossible, or uncertain, or not certain enough."[1] On the other hand, both by precept and example he favored appeals to the authority of the Bible when such appeals seemed useful strategy. In short, as he insisted, the Bible was for the use of the orthodox, and heretics had no right to use it.

So our modern Tertullians use all the logical acumen, philosophical quotations, and every rational device they can muster in their arguments against opposing views. But when others seek to employ the same instruments, they are solemnly reminded that reason is not competent to decide theological issues, and that appeal to rational principles in such matters is a particularly insidious and contemptible form of idolatry.

This looks to the outsider very much like an example of that *ad hoc* rationalization which the revolters are so fond of charging against theologians whose teachings they oppose.

6. *Faith Must Be Commended Either by Word or Example, Either One Being an Appeal to Reason.* The necessity of the believer's witnessing to his faith is acknowledged by all Christians everywhere. But how are we to bear witness to our faith? How shall we commend to those who do not now share it the blessings of the gospel?

We may, of course, do so by telling them of it. If we do we shall have to assume that our hearers are looking for the truth within the testimony which we bear. But if they

[1] *On Prescription against Heretics*, chap. 19.

are doing so they are reasoning, and it is to their reason that we are commending our faith.

Suppose, then, that we remain silent, letting our lives bear testimony to the grace which we have received. Either the observers will be able to see something in our lives to compare with their ideals of what life ought to be and with other lives which have not received the blessings of the gospel, or they will not do so. If they do not make any such comparisons then they will not be recognizing anything attractive or in any sense meaningful or significant in our living testimony. If they do make such comparisons, then it is their comparing activity in search for truth—that is, to their reason—that we are commending the faith.

When it is contended that the recognition of the true way of life is not at all rational, then the ethical content of redemption is implicitly denied. For if the life of the redeemed is morally better than the life of others, then that evidence can be used to favor the true revelation.

In the *Crisis of Faith* Stanley Hopper compares "the Christian standpoint" with the desperate act of a man who is falling into an abyss. As he falls he sees a rope dangling near him. In wild desperation he clutches it and is saved. Such a man does not first insist upon a critical analysis of the rope to find whether it is securely attached and whether by means of it he can return to a place of safety. "He will not, in fact, know whether it will hold him until he has taken hold of it and thrown his weight upon it."[2] He is

[2] *Crisis of Faith*, 183.

desperate and the rope is there. Without further ado he uses it as his means of salvation. So, Dr. Hopper tells us, the man who would be saved from his sin must realize his desperate plight and then seize upon the gospel in the reckless abandon of desperation. To ask critical questions or to make comparisons is to be lacking in utter, self-abandoned commitment and hence in faith, by which alone he might be saved.

Actually, the man of today who is aware of his desperate need is offered not one, but many means of salvation. All about him are dangling ropes clearly labeled as means of rescue. Confronted by communism, scientism and the disciplines of Yoga, how is a man to know which he is to seize? In life, a man has usually a little time in which to make critical judgments. Is he to abandon himself to a capricious choice of the moment? Will his eternal destiny actually depend upon such a choice being the right one? If that is so what must we say of God? Is a mere rewarder of lucky gamblers to be accounted the God of justice? Would such a patron of chance be worthy of eternal veneration and obedience?

7. *Irrationalism Would Turn Back the Clock of Religious Development.* Among the peoples of the world religion began generally in crude and ill-defined forms. Among the savage races practicing the rites of animistic fetishism, it is difficult to distinguish between superstitious magic and the essential beginnings of religion. Step by step, through painful experience, hard-wrought criticism

and prophetic vision, many peoples of the world have advanced far above such levels. In the three centuries between 800 and 500 B.C. there occurred in many parts of the world, almost simultaneously, especially remarkable advances in the rationality and moral quality of religious thought and practice. As George Foot Moore points out,

> This is the age of Taoism in China; of the Upanishads, of Buddhism, and of the precursors of Hinduism in India; of Zoroaster in Iran; of the Orphic-Pythagorean movement in Greece; and of the Hebrew Prophets.[3]

Undoubtedly much of the advance was due to the visions of prophetic seers. However, the appeal which the loftier conceptions had for man was largely based upon the superior reasonableness of the new ideas. Moore describes the evolution of ethical monotheism thus:

> Local and natural religions fuse in national polytheisms; the progress of civilisation in varying degrees moralises religion; mythology and nascent philosophy take up the problem of cosmogony, and are led to unify the creative power or the first principle; the demand for unity in the moral order of the world also tends toward monotheism.[4]

The large place of reason in this development is obvious.

[3] *History of Religions*, Vol. I, viii.
[4] *Ibid.*

Many examples of the appeal to reason in behalf of the nobler faiths are to be found in the literature of the period. Xenophanes ridiculed the absurdity of polytheistic notions with their careless ascription of human bodily characteristics, caprice and immoral motives to the divinities themselves. Scornfully, Heraclitus says,

> And, forsooth, they offer prayers to these statues here! It is as if one should try to converse with houses. They know nothing of the real nature of gods and heroes.[5]

Similarly, Deutero-Isaiah condemns the stupidity of the man who cuts down a tree, uses some of the wood to cook his food,

> and the residue thereof he maketh a god, even his graven image; he falleth down unto it, . . . and saith, Deliver me; for thou art my god.[6]

Significantly, the great prophet continues,

> They know not, neither do they consider: for he hath shut their eyes, that they cannot see; and their hearts, that they cannot understand. And none calleth to mind, neither is there knowledge nor understanding. . . .[7]

[5] Charles M. Bakewell, *Source Book in Ancient Philosophy*, 29.
[6] Isa. 44:17.
[7] Isa. 44:18-19.

If our modern irrationalists would observe how their fore-fathers were taught that high disdain for idolatry which they can now so easily presume as axiomatic, let them read the Greek philosophers and Hebrew prophets and see how much they owe to the critical use of reason! That in such periods of rapid development reason rendered great service to religion can scarcely be doubted.

Likewise, in the history of Christianity, when defenders of the faith have confronted superstitious magic and idola-try, either within or outside the Church, rational criticism has been employed to rebuke these vestiges of barbaric religion and call the faithful to the true way of the gospel. Examples from the early Christian writers and from mod-ern missionary appeals alike, are too numerous to recount.

Are we now to cast aside so useful an alliance as that between reason and ethical monotheism? The results of such a move might not become immediately apparent. But how could the Church deal with new recrudescences of superstition under the guise of Christianity without the aid of reason? If the right of reason to criticize theological doctrine is denied, then no amount of argument that super-stitious practices would be inconsistent with historic Chris-tian doctrine could avail. The defenders of the degenerate rites could reply simply that these inconsistencies were paradoxes and remind the irrationalists that the deepest truths are, according to their own testimony, generally paradoxical.

To reject rational criticism as an instrument for the

discovery of theological truth would be sure, in a short time, to result in religious regression in which all manner of long outgrown absurdity and immorality would return under the guise of paradoxical faith. To interpret the assent of Christian faith as irrational is, as H. D. Lewis says, "a reversal to the mystery-mongering, the cults and priesthoods, of primitive religion."[8]

8. *Christianity Needs the Services of Reason for a Number of Urgent Constructive Tasks.* Not alone for the defense of already hard-won gains does the Christian movement need the assistance of rational procedures. There are a number of tasks pressing hard for attention now which cannot well be performed without the admission of reason to the very heart of theological criticism and judgment.

One of the imperative needs of our time is the restatement of theological doctrines in language meaningful to this age. Such need is not, in principle, new. The whole history of Christian theology is a history of new restatement to bring the revealing God of the Gospels into meaningful communication with people who face new problems and are accustomed to new forms of expression. But never has the need for such restatement been greater than today. While neo-Platonic philosophy, Aristotelian dualism, and the critical method of modern philosophy have all required the reformulation of Christian doctrine, none of these movements of secular thought has been equal in revolu-

[8] *Morals and the New Theology,* 73.

tionary implications to the development of the natural sciences within the last two hundred fifty years. Not only are the scientists and scholars now looking upon a world newly represented in scientific terms. To a large extent, even the most uncritical man on the street thinks and acts in terms of such world views as would have been incredible to the man of five hundred or even two hundred years ago. Modern science has changed the setting in which the gospel must be preached.

It may be protested that the world views which the natural sciences have encouraged are false. But suppose that in some respects this is true. We must then know wherein the truth of the gospel departs from the doctrines which are part and parcel of the prejudices peculiar to our time. It has been often observed that the history of theology is actually the history of the Church's dealings with heresy. The gospel must surely be stated now in terms which are relevant to the scientific ideas of the day. In such restatement, careful distinctions must be made between those ideas occurring among the scientists which are true and welcome and those which a Christian critic must reject. How can such a discriminating task be performed without the aid of reason?

Seven hundred years ago the leaders of Christendom were shocked by the intrusion of Aristotelian philosophy, with its emphasis on empirical observation, on the unreality of independent universals and its critical skepticism of dogmatic deduction. Some defenders of the faith believed that the only proper solution of the crisis would be the flat opposition of the Church to the entire empirical and rational movement. A similar conclusion was actually reached by the leaders of Mohammedanism, and Islam banished the whole of philosophy from the sacred precincts of Allah. The truth of the Koran, they said, was to be accepted, not criticized. The result was a narrowing and hardening of the Mohammedan's religious view of the world and his increasing reliance upon fanatical appeal to violence for the propagation of his ideas.

In Christendom a new counsel finally won the day, and Christianity came to terms with Aristotle. To be sure, the thought of the great Stagirite was revised, but the doctrine of the Church was given powerful and persuasive restatement in terms intelligible within the new intellectual climate.

It would seem tragic if the Church were to fail to speak now in terms capable of being understood by a generation cradled in the lap of science. To fail in that is not to banish the false prejudices of scientism. It is simply to compartmentalize the life of this age. If the healing influence of the gospel is to be felt in the needy world of the twentieth century, the proponents of the gospel must not resort to isolationism. Rather must they enter every market place and laboratory, equipped to expound and defend their message in such a way as to be heard and understood.

Another urgent task which now confronts the Christian thinker is the assimilation of discoveries made by Biblical scholars in recent decades into the system of theological doctrine. Many have been hard at work on this problem and much has been accomplished. All which has been attained has been made possible by rational methods. Even those men who have attacked reason in theology, while employing the instruments of advanced Biblical criticism, have been compelled in practice to acknowledge the requirement that doctrine should be consistent with the evidence.[9] Much remains to be done, both in Biblical criticism and also in relating the historical evidence thus disclosed to present theological thought. If this work is to be done efficiently the worker must know well the instruments with which he works. The division of mind between the suspicion of reason on the one hand and its use on the other only makes for confusion and obscurity.

If there is anything on which all Christians are agreed in our time, it is that certain ethical principles which Jesus taught and exemplified are profoundly needed in the life of humanity today. Supposing that we know what some of these principles are, how shall we be able to understand their implications in practice unless by rational inference? In practice every believer in Christian ethics does continually subsume particular actions under general ethical principles. He sees, for example, that the treatment of workers as mere commodities is contrary to the Christian law of love and hence must not be tolerated. Such deduction is altogether rational. But men suspicious of reason are likely to

[9] See, e.g., Paul S. Minear, "Form Criticism and Faith," *Religion in Life*, Winter Number 1945-1946, pp. 46-56.

make such inferences only when it suits their purposes. On other occasions they can always refuse to admit the validity of the procedure, insisting that the relation between general principle and particular event is a paradoxical one. No one can doubt that such men as Karl Barth and Reinhold Niebuhr have rendered great service in the awakening of multitudes to face critical social problems of our day. However, such men are found invariably to have been trained in earlier years in ethical philosophies making the utmost use of rational criticism in regard both to the definition of universal norms and their application to specific circumstances. Whenever they would apply their ideals to particular requirements of the day they are paying indirect tribute to the rational methods in which they were trained but of which, on other occasions, they express such deep distrust.

At the same time, their strictures against reason blur their own arguments and lend encouragement to the vast number of obscurantists and escapists who are delighted to find that it is quite all right to allow irrational discrepancies within the structure of their moral thought and action. What if they are irrational? Irrationality is the mark of profundity and truth.

How, in terms satisfactory to the revolters, can such escapists be answered except by name-calling or appeal to subtle or overt coercion? Only reason offers a court of non-violent appeal universally intelligible and advantageous to truth.

The discrediting of reason is affecting adversely what Frederic Lilge calls "the crucial problem of education in modern technical civilization—how to prevent the separation of technical power from moral responsibility."[10] Our laboratories have disclosed such power as to bring unparalleled material good within human grasp, but at the same time to threaten all mankind with hitherto unimagined horrors. At this critical juncture the world of science seems lost in a kind of moral paralysis. History has presented no more tragic episode than the present feverish efforts of scientists in many lands to devise new means of self-destruction. Recent years have made it plainer than ever before that, as Joseph L. Hromadka says,

> No civilization can survive without strong faith and conviction; no order of liberty without the eternally valid law; no tolerance without homage before the Truth.[11]

But when the times call for new devotion to good ends, men respond with the invention of new means.

> Man ceased to understand himself and has become helpless in view of an astounding whirlwind. He does not even apprehend the meaning of our times. There is no real knowledge and understanding without definite criteria and norms. There is no life if man

[10] *The Abuse of Learning*, 69.
[11] *Doom and Resurrection*, 28.

does not know in whose name he ought to live and to whose glory he ought to work. There is no freedom without God, without His truth and law.[12]

Now, at this critical time, there comes to the fore a theological movement some members of which deny the possibility of knowing any system of divine law[13] and all of whom are undermining the very means of communication between the theological and scientific communities. How can one relate divinely sanctioned ends to the appropriate political, economic and scientific means if the ends cannot be given explicit rational statement and deductions cannot be drawn from them?

This tragic estrangement between theology and the common life of men in other vocations is made especially acute by the irrational interpretation of moral responsibility. The revolters frequently insist that sin is inevitable but that men are nevertheless responsible for their sin. This is, of course, an irrational paradox, and the favorite example of such a paradox in the teachings of Reinhold Niebuhr. As H. D. Lewis observes,

> The result of this attitude is *to divorce the consciousness of sin and the "uneasy conscience" altogether from the business of living*—a divorce that cannot fail

[12] *Ibid.*, 36.
[13] So Kierkegaard, and so also Barth in his emphatic denial that there can be any Christian ethics, a denial with which Brunner emphatically disagrees.

to have a serious effect upon practice as well as on religious thinking.[14]

There could hardly be a worse time for such a divorce to take place than the present period of world-wide moral crisis.

Another disastrous moral effect of the revolt has been to aggravate the individualism which has so nearly broken down all sense of community, and hence of social responsibility, in our age. The isolation, perplexity and futility of the individual in recent Western civilization, together with the terrible consequences, have been graphically portrayed in such books as Robert L. Calhoun's *God and the Common Life* and Elton Trueblood's *The Predicament of Modern Man*. The psychological barriers between the individual and his fellows are but raised higher by any movement which reduces confidence in that common human rationality which provides the framework of all discourse and the necessary assumption of all intervocational criticism and co-operation.

Frederic Lilge has shown how Kierkegaard, like Nietzsche, helped to shock German academic thought and procedure

out of an often arid preoccupation with technical and departmentalized questions, to restore to its inquiries

[14] *Morals and the New Theology*, 64.

a sense of urgency, and to broaden them so as to include the problems of human existence.[15]

But in doing so he helped prepare that spirit of desperate irrational fanaticism which made the Nazi revolution possible, for

> the very manner in which Kierkegaard defined these problems again so narrowed German existential philosophy that its inquiries ended by isolating the individual hopelessly from society, from humanity, from history, or any rational community of spirits.[16]

To be sure, Kierkegaard's absolute commitment was to God. But once man's choice is reduced to one of irrational despair, there is nothing to deter other existentialists, like Martin Heidegger, from making quite different reckless gambles.

There has been much discussion on the question whether Heidegger's ardent espousal of Nazism was a logical outcome of his existentialism. It is hard to see how there could be *any* logical outcome of such an irrational mood. But the isolated individualism of this position, the lack of a criterion and the disbelief in any discoverable meaning of life did certainly leave his will defenseless against the emotional onslaught of Hitlerism.

[15] *The Abuse of Learning,* 126-127.
[16] *Ibid.*

Such dangers are implicit in the irrationalism of Kierkegaard. Brand Blanshard puts it well.

> Start with the assumption that what God says must
> at least make human sense, and we know what to
> think when some dervish from the desert or from
> Berchtesgaden raises his voice to claim guidance from
> above. Start from the assumption of Kierkegaard,
> Barth and Brunner that revelation must needs be an
> offence to our understanding, and what is to prevent
> us also from becoming blind followers of the blind?[17]

A method and mood which leave men to play the role of
reckless gamblers who may as well choose a blind allegiance
to Christ or to some new anti-Christ ought scarcely to be
encouraged in a world nearly done to death already by
rash adventurers.

[17] Article, "The Inner Light." *The Harvard Divinity School
Bulletin*, XLIII (1946), 63.

CHAPTER FIVE

Reason and Faith

It is apparent that both the revolters and their opponents can make persuasive appeals in behalf of their positions. It would be strange, indeed, if all truth and right in this controversy were to be found on one side. The effort must now be made to discover what are the most important and permanent values which the current theological irrationalism has helped to recover or conserve. Then it will be appropriate to inquire whether these values can be had without incurring the objections which the defenders of reason can rightly make against other aspects of the revolters' position.

A. VALUES IN THE REVOLT

1. *The Rejection of Relativism.* One of the most noteworthy contributions of the irrationalistic movement has been its forthright repudiation of religious relativism in all its forms. For many years a number of intellectual movements have been converging upon a religious conception

strongly reminiscent of Protagoras' dictum, "Man is the measure of all things."

When Albrecht Ritschl restated the great doctrines of salvation as grounded in critical value judgments, he did not mean to encourage a purely subjective interpretation of theism.[1] His emphasis on the faith of the historical community saved him from that. However, in his unfortunately abstract and ponderous style of writing, Ritschl was so positivistic in some of his utterances and so nearly consistent in the employment of terms which could be subjectively interpreted that he became the actual founder of a movement for which he would have had the utmost distaste.

The left-wing Ritschlians have argued that we should not be concerned with the questions of metaphysics. We cannot know what exists apart from our experience. Whether God is or is not, independent of ourselves, is a question beyond the province of human thought. All that we can possibly know is what He means to us. What does God mean in human experience? He means a certain optimistic assurance that the values which we prize most highly will be progressively increased, and that the whole end of our moral life is the participation in a society of brotherly love.

[1] See the unpublished Ph.D. dissertation of E. S. Brightman entitled, "The Criterion of Religious Truth in the Theology of Albrecht Ritschl" (Boston University Graduate School, 1912) for an especially thorough study of the positivistic elements of Ritschl's methodology and a convincing argument that Ritschl did not draw from these elements the skeptical inferences charged by O. Pfleiderer and others.

The subjectivistic interpretation of Ritschl has been combined with the secular philosophy of relativistic pragmatism. As Lovejoy and others have pointed out, pragmatists have often vacillated between the view that practical consequences serve as a useful criterion of truth and the more radical view that practical consequences are the whole meaning of truth. The doctrine that the trueness of an idea is simply its practical usefulness in the fulfillment of human purposes has, when applied to religious belief, a devastating result. When a man who accepts such a pragmatic presupposition says he believes that God exists and that He will by His grace save His people for all eternity, he is only affirming that such a belief is practically helpful for the gaining of certain ends which he desires. God thus becomes a mere projection or symbol of human hopes and aspirations. Such a God is, indeed, an idol created by human thought for human purposes. The harsh words the crisis theologians have uttered against the idolatry of philosophical theism may be truly charged against subjectivistic notions of God.

A third movement in contemporary thought, which has blended in various proportions with the first two, is that psychologism which professes to find in every doctrinal affirmation only an interesting phenomenon of human behavior or feeling. Undoubtedly it is quite legitimate to ask on occasion what have been the emotional or behavioral accompaniments of any given creedal formulation. But there is another kind of question which is of greater concern to man as man, namely, the question of the truth or falsehood embodied in the creed. Some psychologically oriented students would disavow completely the significance of this latter question. The only inquiry worth launching concerning any human thought, they say, concerns its psychological antecedents and consequences. For such thinkers God is only a psychological event in a man.

The author remembers vividly a classroom of his college days in which a lecturer in philosophy stated, "There are as many gods as there are people. For every man has his own god." When one of his students inquired whether he did not mean merely that there were as many *ideas* of God as there were people, he replied, "It is all the same thing."

With such views the revolters come into the sharpest conflict by insisting that God is not ourselves nor any part of ourselves, nor are we any part of Him. He is Wholly Other. Regrettable as it appears to many thinkers that the phrase "Wholly Other" is often interpreted as meaning *absolutely* different in *kind,* every genuine believer in an independently existing God welcomes the scorn which the revolters heap upon the superficial psychologizers who take from words all meaning beyond the context of merely human events.

A fourth type of relativism often influenced by the first three is the identification of the meaning of theological ideas with their history in human thought. Shirley Jackson

Case is an especially well-known exponent of such a view. For example, he points out that Christians delight in singing, "O Thou who changest not, abide with me," and then he adds, "Are we justified in thinking that religion and Christianity in particular, is a stable, permanent and unchanging phenomenon?"[2] One might as well quote an astronomer's statement that the distance of the moon from the earth had not changed measurably in the last thousand years, and then ask whether it was actually true that men's ideas on the subject had not changed in ten centuries!

A large part of Case's writing is devoted to the instructive task of showing the social contexts in which various Christian doctrines and movements have come into historical existence. If he were content with providing such background for the examination of theological teaching, no one ought to object. But when he goes further, as he sometimes does, and suggests that the meaning of theological ideas is identical with their human history he denies what is the very essence of the Christian faith. Again, every believer who prays to a God who is the very Creator of man, the supreme Legislator of the moral law and the Author of our salvation, welcomes the insistence of the crisis theologians on the unconditioned and absolute being of God.

2. *The Refusal to Limit God's Being to the Bounds of Our Knowledge.* The dependence upon reason requires

[2] *Christianity in a Changing World*, 6.

the thinker to prefer hypotheses which he can precisely understand to those which leave wide margins of vagueness and uncertainty. Moreover, the rationalist generally supposes that he ought not to believe more than the facts will prove. The proof must, of course, appear in terms understandable to human reason. A resulting tendency among rationalists, therefore, is to limit God's being to the capacities of our understanding fully to comprehend. More than that, the rationalist may be tempted to think of God as confined to the limits of man's actual knowledge. Put so baldly, such a proposition would be denied by most thinkers. Yet a believer in reason who is candid will be compelled, I think, to admit the temptation to limit his belief in such fashion.

On the other hand, experience shows that such a limitation of God is actually absurd. Every advance of human thought about God is an indication that the previous thoughts concerning Him were inadequate. The vast range of unexplained mysteries in the world indicates that there is much more of truth yet needed before man can have even an approximately adequate conception of God's being.

The current reaction against belief in reason has included much emphasis on the vast unknown areas in the being and activity of God. Such reminders of the fragmentary and primitive character of our knowledge are wholesome and true. Sir Isaac Newton was properly humble before the vast realm of unknown truth. Said he,

I do not know what I may appear to the world; but to myself I seem to have been only like a boy playing on the seashore, and diverting myself in now and then finding a smoother pebble or a prettier shell than ordinary, whilst the great ocean of truth lay all undiscovered before me.[3]

More recent scientists who have been working on the frontier of knowledge have given witness to similar impressions. Can the religious thinker content himself with a lesser intellectual humility when confronted by the illimitable mystery and power of Him who has made all things?

Some rationalists may protest that in urging such humility the revolters are recommending what every rationalist has always taken for granted. It may, therefore, be useful to take an example of a rationalistic view of God which illustrates the kind of limitation which the revolters attack.

One of the most persistent and brilliant efforts in modern philosophy of religion to penetrate the purposes and being of God by human reason is the "theistic finitism" of Edgar S. Brightman. As he has confronted the vast range and variety of meaningful value in the world, Dr. Brightman has seen abundant evidence of God's existence. On the other hand, as he has observed the terrible grip of evil upon the life of the world, it has seemed to him evident that God's power must be limited by some obstruction or

[3] Christopher Morley, ed., *Familiar Quotations by John Bartlett,* 184.

inadequacy within Himself, making it impossible for Him to realize fully His purpose that only good should come forth.

In past centuries most theologians confronted with the problem of evil have resolved it in part by observing the manifold ways in which the most frightful evils have been shown capable of serving good ends. If man be regarded as a being whom God has created to share with Him the creative and responsible life of freedom, then moral evil or sin may be attributed to man, and God will be relieved of responsibility for it. Such natural evil as may then be observed in the world may be regarded as part of the best possible world in which sinful and perverse human wills may be purged of evil and taught to follow the path of righteousness and peace. There was a time when Professor Brightman was himself deeply impressed by such explanations.[4] In those days, he believed that the natural evils not thus far explainable as intended for morally good purpose were akin to those events in nature which the scientist had found himself temporarily unable to bring within the province of causal law. When experience had become richer and man had studied more deeply, the rationality of both kinds of events could be confidently expected to show itself.

But when other thinkers profess to believe in such explanations, Professor Brightman now accuses them of appeals to ignorance.[5] So long as we do not see and under-

[4] Cf. his *An Introduction to Philosophy* (1925), 332-333.
[5] E.g., in *A Philosophy of Religion* (1940), 309-310.

stand how some aspects of human experience can possibly be employed to bring forth good, we should frankly admit them to be surd evils, he says. By surd evil he means an evil which "is not in any sense an instrumental good."[6] Accordingly, rather than admit any limitation inherent in man's reasoned knowledge as accounting for our failure to understand such apparently senseless evils, he attributes the lack of rationality to the nonrational Given in God Himself.

Against such projection of confusion and frustration within our own experience into the being of God Himself, the revolters against reason would make vigorous protest. In doing so they would call us back to the view which is obviously predominant in the Scriptures and in Christian tradition.

Had the ancient Hebrews believed in a nonrational Given within God as the ultimate explanation of evil they would have been saved much of their most anguished thought and prayer. The Psalmist then would never have cried out, "My God, my God, why hast Thou forsaken me?"[7] He would have been saved from such struggle by the belief that God was simply unable to prevent his suffering.[8] Neither would the prophets of the exile have labored with the problem of God's apparent neglect of His chosen people. But the world would have lost those deeper treasures of faith and of thought which flowed from the hard-won

[6] *Ibid.*, 246.
[7] Ps. 22:1.
[8] Cf. Brightman, *A Philosophy of Religion*, 246.

insight that through the most tragic suffering the highest good may come, that even though nearly all of a people may perish, the purged remnant may be the medium through which may be won the supreme triumph of God and man.

Likewise, if St. Paul had attributed the unexplained injustice apparent to human experience as due to a non-rational Given in God, he would have been saved his years of soul-searching on the meaning of the Cross. What could have been more evident to him than that the humiliation, suffering and death of God's Messiah, the son of the divine Father, were due simply to the fact that God's power was unable to prevent this calamity? He might then have shrugged his shoulders and looked to the future in the effort to retrieve whatever values were possible in spite of the calamity which had occurred.

But such a way was not open to Paul. He assumed that God did have power to prevent such evils. He assumed, therefore, that the apparent irrationality of the Cross, a stumbling block to the Jews and an affront to the reason of the Greeks, was evidence of man's limitations of understanding and of God's mysterious transcendence. In prayer and intense spiritual suffering, Paul sought for a deeper understanding of this mystery of mysteries. It is because he had faith that man's rational powers were limited by sin, rather than that God's will was limited by any sort of obstruction, that the Cross has become to millions the symbol of divine love and of triumph over all evil. A similar humility on our part may prevent the imprisonment of our own spirits in the narrow confines of a theory which upholds faith in human reason at the expense of limiting imagination and faith in God.[9]

3. *The Condemnation of Sophisticated Indecision.* For many years a serious bane of the more educated classes has been the tendency of the best minds to withdraw from man's heaviest responsibilities.

Dr. Thomas Briggs of Teachers College, Columbia University, asked his students and an additional group of men selected by them as "cultured persons," to tell which ones among ninety-eight suggested traits were compatible with personal culture. Ninety-six per cent declared that a cultured person was not "dogmatic and assertive of his opinions." Moreover, "it was found, on tabulation, that no other trait among the 98 listed was so widely regarded as incompatible with genuine culture."[10] Dr. Briggs' experiment is further evidence of that paralysis of the will which many men have observed as a kind of occupational disease in the academic community. In many societies of educated men it is considered much more praiseworthy to discover objections to every possible course of action than to act and risk the consequences of failure.

Many a scholar who might have devoted his powers to

[9] Cf. Nels F. S. Ferré, *Evil and the Christian Faith.* For an excellent criticism of Dr. Brightman's "finitistic" theory as a whole, see Albert C. Knudson, *The Doctrine of God,* 272-275 and *The Doctrine of Redemption,* 204-212.

[10] Arthur E. Murphy, *The Uses of Reason,* 93.

the salvation of himself and of other men, has actually spent his life in perpetual weighing of the pros and cons relative to every proposed decision. The scientifically trained mind shrinks from the "crime of easy belief." He must seek sufficient evidence to be sure before he commits himself. However, in important matters the crucial evidence seems never to be completely in. So the puzzling appraisal of evidence goes on endlessly. The very task of appraisal itself becomes a kind of game, the excitement of which furnishes its own reward. The end of the road is never reached and decisions in fundamental matters never made. Our universities are full of both professors and students who would prefer to speculate and argue about the existence of God and the way of salvation, rather than to commit themselves with full responsibility to any course of practical religious devotion. Sophisticated indecision has become for many both a satisfying pastime and a soul-destroying vice.

Against this vice such men as Kierkegaard and Barth have sounded the alarm. In so doing they have rendered an important service. For, whatever truth a thinker may envision in the course of his study, he will never make that truth a means of redemption, either for himself or for any other, until he makes decisive commitment to it. The sure way to miss making one's life count for truth is the failure to commit oneself to any belief. Greater than the "crime of easy belief" is the crime of unbelief. Only less vicious in degree than unbelief is faint, half-hearted belief.

For men of little faith will never win the future for truth. In the judgment of the ages, it is better to be either hot or cold than to be lukewarm.

The revolters have reminded us once again of the truth that salvation is by faith, by wholehearted self-commitment, not by reason. There is hardly a lesson more in need of learning.

4. The Observation That Our Reason Is Dependent upon Faith. The men who have led the recent assault upon reason have recalled to mind that even reason itself cannot stand alone. The fact is that without faith reason can do nothing.[11] Indeed, there are a number of commitments which must be made by faith before reason can make any advance toward the knowledge of reality.

(a) For example, if our reason is to give us any truth about the realm of existence, we must have an initial faith that there is an inherent kinship between that bias toward the meaningful and systematic which James called the sentiment of rationality, on the one hand, and universal being on the other. If no such kinship is actually present,

---

[11] Here the word "faith" is used in its broader sense, to mean a commitment beyond the limits of rationally established certainty. Christian faith, the Kierkegaardians would insist, is a different matter altogether. As to its comprehensiveness, causation, results, and, above all, its object, it certainly is a unique kind of faith. Nevertheless, it does appear to belong in the genus of faith as here broadly defined. Moreover, as Augustine showed, the kinds of faith we are discussing here actually imply belief in God. Compare Kant's principle of "the primacy of the practical reason" and also Whitehead's comment quoted on p. 178 n.

then the constructions which our reason elaborates upon the material of experience may give no clue to the meanings of existence itself.

(b) Not only must the effective rationalist have faith in the kinship between reason and reality. He must also commit himself unreservedly to those basic moral obligations on which all knowledge rests. A strange though common phenomenon is a scientist who denies the validity of ethics. Moral principles he regards as mere conventions or preferences, unrelated to the fundamental structure of that reality which is independent of human thought and feeling. Yet this same scientist will know, if he takes the trouble to look, that apart from faith in the inherent superiority of honesty over dishonesty, of patience over impatience, of faithful discipline over uncontrolled caprice, not one segment of the scientific structure which he has reared would have any claim to the acceptance of men. The entire structure of human knowledge rests upon certain basic moral convictions. Ethical faith is prior to rational understanding.

(c) Moreover, all the work of science depends upon faith in the value of certain kinds of experience. If the examined life is no better than the unexamined, if science is no better than superstition, then no one need trouble himself with the arduous tasks of intellectual search for truth. Only faith in the value of truth will make possible its actual achievement. The belief in certain kinds of value also plays an important role within the process of critical inquiry. The intuition of rational symmetry is at bottom

177

closely akin, at least, to an aesthetic intuition[12] and is equally an intuition of value. Without faith in the validity of such insights reason would be helpless, even in logic and mathematics, to say nothing of the search for truth about existing reality.

When it comes to using reason in the search for truth about God and human destiny, faith in value experience plays an even more important role. Unless one believes that some kinds of conduct are better than others, that some kinds of sense experience are more beautiful than others, that some dedications of soul are more right than others, then whatever evidence may be found for belief in a First Cause or a coldly impersonal Mind, no evidence can be adduced for the existence of a good God, much less of such a One as the loving Father of our Lord Jesus Christ. All of the rational arguments for the existence of the Christian's God rest upon faith in moral and other values.

B. THE VALIDITY OF REASON

While we have acknowledged a number of positive values resulting from the revolt against reason, we must still protest against its depreciation of reason itself. In Chapter Three we considered the weaknesses in the charges against

[12] Cf. Whitehead's statement, "The metaphysical doctrine, here expounded, finds the foundations of the world in the aesthetic experience. . . . All order is therefore aesthetic order. . . . The actual world is the outcome of the aesthetic order, and the aesthetic order is derived from the immanence of God." *Religion in the Making*, 104-105.

reason and in Chapter Four a number of positive objections to irrationalism. Those considerations are unaffected by the acknowledgment of certain useful emphases of the revolt.

There seems to be no escape from the necessity of assuming the validity of reason and using it continually in all meaningful life. It is only by dependence upon our human rational powers that we can understand the meaning of any proposition whatsoever, no matter from what transcendent revelation it may have come. At no point can a line be consistently drawn between the understanding of the meaning and implications of a proposition about existence and the understanding of the grounds upon which it rests. However inadequate it may be, our own thinking capacity is all that we have for the interpretation of our total experience, revelatory or otherwise.

The disbelief in reason, although it has given rise to many good influences along the way, is fundamentally self-contradictory. The irrationalist cannot escape being caught on the horns of his great dilemma, to be consistently irrational or not. If he is not, then his distrust of reason is not thoroughgoing. If he is consistently irrational, he will be so only by disciplined effort in obedience to his conviction that such consistency may be rightly demanded of him. In the latter event he will be paying high tribute to the valid claims of reason to rule the thought of man. In either case, then, irrationalism must be halfhearted and incapable of standing upon its own foundations. This halfheartedness cannot be dissipated by any amount of dramatic denunciation or violent assertion. All the meaning which irrationalism can possess it must receive from its implicit deference to reason.

If the revolter seeks to keep his irrationalism narrowly confined within the area of thought about man's eternal destiny and the being and nature of God, he will be doomed to such compartmentalizing of his own life as will leave his religion quite disconnected from the affairs of every day. At the same time, all meaning in his religious beliefs themselves will be derived from his own rational interpretation, however large a role revelation may have played in the experience interpreted.

We seem, ourselves, to have been brought now into the presence of a dilemma. The revolt against reason has brought to our attention a number of practical values and important truths which we should like to embrace. At the same time the revolt itself seems essentially unsound. The question, then, now presents itself whether we can have the positive values of the revolt without falling victim to its fatal defects.

Must reason be repudiated in order to affirm the positive values we have discovered in the revolt against it?

C. REASON ITSELF REQUIRES ACCEPTANCE
OF THE VALUES IN THE REVOLT

Upon careful examination, reason will be found not to oppose, but actually to require, the acceptance of those values which have been here presented under the banner of irrationalism.

1. The religious relativism which the revolters have so strenuously attacked is self-contradictory, and therefore quite contrary to the most basic principle of human reason. If every theological proposition is merely a projection of certain human emotions—that is to say, is a rationalization in the current psychological sense—then this doctrine that every theological proposition is such a projection is itself a mere rationalization. For this doctrine is itself a theological proposition. If every belief in moral principle is but a prejudice of an individual or group, then the belief in such honesty and self-discipline as have led some men to affirm such moral relativism are themselves mere subjective preferences without inherent claim to superiority. In short, if moral relativism is true, then its truth destroys every argument by which it might be known to be true.

On the other hand, if the hypothesis that certain ideal norms of value are valid, quite apart from human preferences and opinions, is examined thoughtfully, much evidence will be found to support it. It is possible to construct a highly systematic rational structure of moral law.[13] Moreover such a system of ideal norms can be shown to be profoundly related to the world of existence. Such relatedness occurs principally in two forms.

First, there is the fact that only by the acceptance of a

[13] E.g., see E. S. Brightman, *Moral Laws;* and W. R. Sorley, *Moral Values and the Idea of God.*

number of such norms can many truths about the world be established. This is the relation which we have observed when speaking of the moral faith implicit in the work of the scientist.

Second, human beings with their inherent and inescapable interest in ideals and their applications do actually exist. Whatever else the world may be, it is a kind of world which actually produces beings who discipline themselves by their concern with ideals of value.

Since relativism is self-contradictory and the belief in ideal norms of value has much evidence to support it, reason itself requires the rejection of relativism. It may be observed further that many believers in reason as instrument of religious knowledge have steadfastly opposed relativism all through the years. Among them are such varied thinkers as Clement of Alexandria, Thomas Aquinas, Hegel, Borden Parker Bowne and Wilbur F. Urban.

2. It has been admitted that rationalists are tempted to limit God's being to the bounds of human knowledge and that rationalists occasionally succumb to this temptation. However, it must now be insisted that when they do so succumb, it is because their reasoning is itself one-sided. Reason requires the taking into account of all data available. Belief which is neatly circumscribed, admitting minimal margins of mystery, is true to the rational demand for internal consistency and harmony, but it is often false to the equally important rational demand for admission into account of all experience. The fact is that there are many

experiences which even the most penetrating human mind is unable specifically to explain.

For example, we may give a general account of the most unjustly evil aspects of experience as due to divine rational purposes not yet adequately unfolded to us; but we cannot go on to tell exactly why they have not been unfolded nor what significance they will be found to have when the meaning does come to be more fully understood.

If such evil elements in human life be attributed to a nonrational Given in God, it may seem that a more precise and understandable explanation has been provided, for if the cause of these elements be nonrational then their nonrational character may appear to be sufficiently accounted for. However, such an impression is illusory. Actually the meaning of an event is not one whit further explained when it has been attributed to the Given, but then the very possibility of any explanation ever being found has been denied. For all explanation implies intelligibility. What is inherently nonrational can neither be intelligible within itself nor can any inference be made from its existence regarding the causation of such and such further events.

We are not here objecting to the doctrine of a nonrational Given merely because evils are not explainable by necessary rational deduction from it. There are other rational modes of explanation besides deductive inference.

My wife recently gave me a phonograph recording of "The Hallelujah Chorus" from Händel's "Messiah." This gift is altogether intelligible. It did not, however, follow by rational necessity from any previously true propositions about reality. In the actual selection of the record and the giving of it, there was a creative act of intelligence and love which could not be deduced from prior realities. But the gift is in understandable relations with the donor's thoughtful affection, my fondness for such music, the existence of such a recording, and our possession of a phonograph.

According to Professor Brightman's theory, there are aspects of the world which are not explainable in any such ways as these. They are nonrational, surd evils which have always been in God's nonrational Given and hence must of necessity be also in our experience. But never are we told what these surds are, nor is any reason given why their existence in God makes it necessary for Him to project them into the experience of man. If any explanation were to be given, it would presumably have to be an explanation in terms of causation or of some analogous kind of necessary connection. But causality and all other experiences of "form" Dr. Brightman would attribute to God's "uncreated eternal reason."[14] Since the nonrational Given is, by hypothesis, neither in the "eternal reason," nor an expression of it, nor "ratified"[15] by it, it is hard to see how it can be within the framework of causal law or any other kind of intelligible connection. Can anything, then, be a necessary

[14] See his *Philosophy of Religion*, 321.
[15] *Ibid.*, 303.

effect of it? But if nothing in our experience is an effect of the nonrational Given, then what evidence can we have that such a Given exists?

Only so long as a thinker believes that ultimately all experience is grounded in a Being completely intelligible to His own reason can rational inquiry hope to continue indefinitely advancing in the search for truth. Reason itself, therefore, dictates that apparent irrationalities in our experience should be attributed to our ignorance, which is inherently capable of being progressively overcome, and not to a fundamental nonrationality in God which will forever, and of necessity, leave some aspects in experience unexplainable. In this one respect Kierkegaard has in the name of revolt against reason been more rationalistic than have such "rationalists" as Dr. Brightman. Kierkegaard at least believes that to God all is rational. In that belief is ground for the rationalist's hope of increasing understanding, even in areas where obscurity and mystery still cloud our view.

3. We have observed with gratitude the revolters' insistence that a man should make definite commitment of his life rather than remain in perpetual consideration of alternatives. But this belief is by no means peculiar to the irrationalist. Indeed, thinking rationally, we can see that indecision is sure to lose whatever values there may be in truth. A man who commits himself to what seems to him probable may, of course, miss the way of true wisdom. But if he fails to commit himself to anything, he is sure to miss that

way. To believe that A is probable and yet to act as if one did not believe in A is to be unreasonable. When one is confronted with a forced and momentous option, being under the necessity of commitment either to A or to B, then if A seems more probable, reason dictates that one should follow course A with all the energy of which one is capable. To fail in this is to betray the fundamental principle of reason, namely, the earnest search for truth. Belief in God is a forced and momentous option, as William James showed. We are not concerned here with James's dubious teaching that the pragmatic advantages of affirmative faith constitute sufficient justification of it in such a dilemma. We are concerned with the overwhelming reasonableness of committing ourselves decisively to this momentous belief, which rational evidence sustains as more probably true than any known alternative.

4. The irrationalists have been emphatic in their insistence that reason is unable to stand alone. This discovery is actually open to reason itself. Indeed, it is by the rational examination of man's thinking procedure that his dependence upon faith has been discovered.[16] Since reason requires the consideration of all possible data of experience, it requires the admission of its own dependence upon faith. This is not to be regarded as a weakness of reason any more than the dependence of salvation upon faith is a weakness of salvation. It is simply a due recognition of the role which reason rightfully plays in human life.

[16] Cf. pp. 58-59, 176-178.

D. KINDS OF REASON

Near the beginning of our study we observed that Kierke-gaard had used the word "reason" in the broadest sense, to mean any human activity directed by the purpose to discover truth. In our own examination of the objections to reason in religion and in our countercharges against irrationalism, it has not been necessary to make more than incidental reference to the various kinds of reason. But now attention must be directed to some important distinctions. In our present constructive task we must observe that various kinds of reason have radically different relations to faith.

We shall not undertake here an exhaustive classification. It will suffice to distinguish five truth-seeking procedures which, in various ways, are especially significant for faith.

1. One of the most exacting intellectual ideals ever conceived is the notion of a philosophy of which no part could be doubted without self-contradiction. One cannot but admire Descartes for wishing to bring into the confusions and conflicts of philosophical thought that certainty and steady progress which he knew so well in mathematics.

Descartes followed in the steps of Augustine when he insisted that it was impossible to doubt the proposition, "I think," since obviously to assert doubt is to affirm, "I think [doubtfully]." But unlike Augustine he then endeavored to derive his view of all being by strict deduction from that simple *Cogito*. The attempt was foredoomed to failure, as was the similar "geometrical method" of Spinoza. Descartes started from a base so narrow as to be quite incapable of bearing the weight placed upon it. Spinoza, on the other hand, assumed so much at the outset that from the very beginning his postulates were open to the gravest doubts.

We owe to Descartes and Spinoza a great debt for having done much to break the power of medieval authoritarianism and to inaugurate the modern spirit of free inquiry. But while we applaud their intellectual daring, we cannot approve their specific method. No one now cares to renew their experiment, unless it be the logical positivists who do so only to demonstrate its futility. Indeed, the idea of using their rationalistic method as the means of establishing a philosophical system would be of little more than historical interest, if theologians did not seem to assume, at times, that all defenders of reason believed in it. When the revolters denounce the philosophers who think that by "reason alone" they can find the truth, they must be haunted by the specter of Cartesian intellectual asceticism. For every other conception of reason makes the very phrase, "reason alone," an absurdity. Every type of rational method employed by any philosopher of religion living today requires that reason should not be "alone," but that it should be at work with the data provided in experience. The data are not given by reason, even in the broad sense of truth-seeking activity, but are thrust upon us by independent, active existents, which affect us in all kinds of ways, whether we seek truth or not.

Certainly no Cartesian consistency nor "geometrical method" is a sufficient guide in determining the valid content of faith. But it seems hardly necessary for theologians to spend time today in fighting a ghost so long laid to rest.

2. Among the many intellectual pursuits of mankind, the one in which most progress has been achieved in our age is the scientific study of the physical world. So spectacular are the discoveries of the scientists and so radically have they revolutionized our daily lives that when the common man hears of "progress" or "civilization" or even "the abundant life," he thinks immediately of automobiles and penicillin, airplanes and television. It is small wonder that in our time "proof" should mean to many minds demonstration by laboratory experiment, and that "reason" should be identified with the procedures of the natural sciences or only slightly broadened to include the analogous methods of the social sciences.

If the beliefs of the inquirer about God and human destiny are to be limited to the propositions verifiable by these "scientific" methods, then he will emerge, not only with no doctrine of God, but also with no moral convictions whatsoever. Ironically, he will also be compelled, in the end, to give up some doctrines on which the sciences themselves rest.

The inadequacy of scientific method as universal test of truth, and specifically in matters of ethics and religion, is due to several limitations.

First of all, the scientist seeks explanation through analysis of the complex and heterogeneous wholes of experience into small, and, as far as possible, exactly similar units. Thus he explains matter in terms of protons and electrons, music is reduced to waves of rarefaction and condensation occurring in measurable amplitude and wave length, while the character of the individual is explained by neural impulses, conditioned reflexes, hormones and genes.

Analysis is extremely useful for the discovery of repetitive aspects in our experience. It is precisely such elements which are of primary concern to the scientist. For the causal laws which he seeks are invariably repeated orders of sequence. So far as there is in a situation a genuine novelty, an emergence of a new meaning or a new level of being, that constitutes for the scientist an unsolved problem. The problem can be solved scientifically only so far as the new can be shown to be not new but a repetition of something old. If there is actually irreducible novelty there, say in the emergence of a new species by mutation or in the painting of an original masterpiece, that novelty is either "explained away" by a false reduction or left as a kind of surd with which science can have nothing more to do.

Now it is precisely creation which gives evidence of a Creator. Any event whatsoever which would give evidence that the world was not a mere machine but the expression of a purposive Mind would have to contain in it some truly new aspect, not a mere repetition of what had been before. Since such novelty cannot be explained as repetition, that is, as an instance of causal law, it must be explained, if at all, by a creative principle. Both the teleological argument, in all its valid forms, and the evidences of particular revelatory experiences of God are cases in point. Even the entire system of causal order itself may be regarded as such a novel event, against the background of a hypothetical time of its nonexistence. In that case, the very existence of a causal system may be taken as an evidence of a cosmic purpose and hence of God.

But when evidences of purpose are found in novel emergents, even though an eminent biologist and mathematician statistically proves the impossibility of any mechanistic, non-purposive explanation of them, as has been done recently by du Noüy,[17] the demonstration is widely regarded as a speculative philosophical study not strictly scientific.

Scientific analysis is invaluable for the performance of many tasks. It is highly useful as one stage in the study of every problem with which the religious man is concerned. But it is weakest at the very point where faith has most at stake, namely, the discovery of worth-while ends and of divine creative acts performed for the sake of those ends. It is weak here because the discovery of ends and the relations of means to them requires the study of wholes as wholes, with special attention to their unique, unrepeated meanings.

Closely related to the emphasis on analysis is the scientific effort to reduce all qualitative description to quantitative accounts. The ancient Pythagorean explanation of all things in terms of number repeats itself in modern physics

[17] In his *Human Destiny*.

and chemistry, while even the sociologist or psychologist is likely to be considered unscientific until his descriptions can be translated into statistical tables. It will be readily conceded that modern empirical measurements are far more exact and that modern mathematics is incomparably more adequate to the task than were those of the Pythagoreans. It is equally evident that such description of all physical being in terms of pure mathematics as Sir James Jeans presents in his excellent book, *Physics and Philosophy,* is exceedingly useful for purposes of prediction and control. There are aspects of experience which constantly repeat themselves and it is precisely these uniformities of nature which are of concern to science. But as description of a concrete, dynamic world in which there is real time and movement, the modern Pythagorean reduction of all to discrete, identical units is subject to the same kinds of criticism which Zeno made of its ancient counterpart, and more besides. Both the usefulness and the ultimate inaccuracy of the scientific reduction of a qualitatively creative real duration to mere quantitative terms have been thoroughly explained by Henri Bergson in *Creative Evolution* and *Time and Free Will.*

One of the first casualties of this scientific reduction is the experience of value. Such contrasting data as the beautiful and ugly, good and bad disappear in the scientific mode of explanation. Science prides itself on being objective, not only in the sense of being unbiased, but also in the sense of keeping clear of all evaluation excepting the abstractly intellectual. In his determination to learn what are the facts, the scientist disciplines himself to ignore their value or evil. This is quite proper within the narrow confines of his important, abstract task. But experience of value remains, whether ignored or not. Indeed, if it did not and if distinctions of value were not taken seriously, science and superstition would be on equal footing as actual phenomena of human society.[18]

The evaluation of experience is especially important for ethics and religion. If all such concepts as pain and pleasure, sin and righteousness, guilt and holiness were ignored, morals and religion would cease to exist, along with the study of them in ethics and philosophy of religion. Description of morals and religion can be made without explicit evaluation. But morals then become mere mores, and religion is reduced to a subjective or social phenomenon, the objective reference of both being lost to view. The dynamic reality of both the real obligation[19] of the moral life and the actual communion with a transcendent God in religion are not discernible by the scientific observer as such. The question whether they are, indeed, real cannot even be asked without leaving behind the boundaries of scientific method.

Finally, it must be noted that science weights the data of sense perception. It can no longer be said that scientists believe only in the reality of the seen. It would be more nearly true to say that as scientists they now believe only

[18] Cf. pp. 177-178.
[19] The *real* obligation spoken of here must not be confused with the mere *feeling* of obligation.

in the reality of the unseen. Certainly such entities as time-space, electrons and Planck's constant are well beyond the range of the senses. But scientists are generally committed to accept as *evidence* only data which can be publicly examined. This is usually taken to mean the data of sense perception. It will be recalled that this was the ground of John B. Watson's pronouncement, in his *Behaviorism*, that the scientist should deny the existence of consciousness.

Now faith is not only concerned primarily with unseen *objects*, such as God and the soul. It is also grounded to a large extent upon *evidences* which appear to the inner life of the spirit, such as the experiences of aspiration, guilt and divine love. As Augustine saw so clearly, man's whole search for truth, which, of course, would include modern science, depends upon belief in the validity of some of these private inner experiences, most of all the imperative lure of perfection. But although the sciences rest upon faith that honesty is better than dishonesty, and disciplined loyalty to ideal truth is imperative, they are, as sciences, unable to discover it, just as a man cannot see the visual sensorium in his own brain, although all the seeing he does is done by means of it.

Scientific reason is based on faith. But it cannot evaluate that faith nor the more inclusive faith of the Christian.

3. Another conception of reason which is more obviously incapable of making a fair appraisal of religious beliefs is that of a reason which, however philosophical and compre-

hensive in other respects, is by definition or assumption opposed to revelation.

In discussions of reason, clergymen often begin by speaking of "reason" and "revelation" as mutually exclusive terms. Similarly, some naturalistic philosophers assume from the start that belief in revelation is a mere projection of desire, an uncritical superstition or a product of forces at work solely within the limits of human society. The delusions of revelation would therefore be contrasted with the enlightenment of reason. The first chapter of John Dewey's book, *A Common Faith*, is a case in point.

Obviously, if the validity of revelation-claims from any source is to be examined by any rational method, the inquiry must be open-minded. A judgment prejudiced by arbitrary initial predication is not a judgment rendered by reason.

4. The fourth kind of reason incapable of the partnership with faith which our study to this point has demanded is appeal to the internal coherence of a limited system. Some of the criticisms which Kierkegaard makes of Hegel, especially in *The Concept of Dread*, seem to imply that the Dane understood the Hegelian principle of coherence to be of this sort. Regarding the method of "Hegel and his school," he writes as follows:

> In logic they use *the negative* as the motive power which brings movement into everything. And movement in logic they must have, any way they can get it,

by fair means or foul. The negative helps them, and if the negative cannot, then quibbles and phrases can, just as the negative itself has become a play on words. In logic no movement can *come about*, for logic is, and everything logical simply is.[20]

It is a temptation to digress for a defense of Hegel against this charge. For although Hegel's dialectic does creak at the joints occasionally, lacking, in practice, quite sufficient flexibility for adaptation to all the demands of an infinitely varied experience, he nevertheless includes within his system a vast amount of empirical observation and means to take into account all the empirical data possible.[21] Kierkegaard seems never to take this empirical side of Hegel adequately into account. But we must not stray from our chosen task. Hegel's condescending treatment of religion is, in any event, indefensible, and our concern is not with him but with the truth about reason and faith.

In principle, at least, Hegel knew well that the internal consistency and even the closely knit coherence of a tight little system would be no guarantee of its truth. The shaft of Oliver Wendell Holmes's ironical "Logic is logic; that's all I say,"[22] cannot be aimed at him. In Hegel's view the whole of reality is process.[23] The body of knowledge, like the whole of reality, is dynamic. Any new event or observa-

[20] *The Concept of Dread,* 11-12.
[21] This is especially evident in *Phänomenologie des Geistes.*
[22] Last line of "The Deacon's Masterpiece."
[23] *Encyclopädie,* Section 577.

tion which refuses to fit in the present system compels revision and may require revolutionary reconstruction.[24]

As Bergson has so beautifully shown in his *Two Sources of Morality and Religion*, a vital and creative faith is unalterably opposed to a closed system of thought. So is the love of truth. The sincere searcher after truth can never bear to refuse consideration to any datum. The new observation may be hard on complacency, but it may also bring truth undreamed of before. In religious terms, the heart and mind of the devotee of Truth must be always hospitable, for he may entertain angels unawares.

5. The rational method which seems most adequate for universal application is that type of synoptic method which appeals to unlimited comprehensive coherence.[25] Those who employ this test of truth try every hypothesis for both consistency with, and relevance to, all possible observed data and previously adopted theories. The effort is continually made to construct the system of knowledge which includes the widest possible variety of data. This is done by means of constant search for more data, revision of previously held theories, and the postulating of new explanatory hypotheses.

Some problems, to be sure, belong within limited uni-

[24] It is worth noting that it was this open empiricism in Hegel's method which especially appealed to the revolutionary thought of Lenin though Hegel would have been horrified at Lenin's use of it. See Lenin, *Teachings of Karl Marx*, 14, and *Religion*, 34. Also V. Marcu, *Lenin*, 47.

[25] Cf. Brightman, *An Introduction to Philosophy* and *A Philosophy of Religion*.

verses of discourse. The question, what is the square root of 64, can be settled without reference to the color of robins' eggs. Arithmetic is an elaborate analysis of certain concepts of quantity. One arithmetical solution follows from another with logical necessity. For example, if the square of 8 is 64, then the square root of 64 *must* be 8. In this instance the requirement of consistency is so imperatively clear that breadth of relevance is comparatively unimportant. However, the fact that the square root of 64 has such a wide range of applicability, for example, in electrical engineering and astronomy, does give to it and to the whole system of arithmetical propositions of which it is a part an augmented significance. Even if the fact that $\sqrt{64}=8$ is no truer than the fact that Lewis Carroll's Baker met a Boojum Snark, the mathematical proposition is a much more important and deeply rooted truth. In both instances the comprehensive criterion of coherence can be appealed to for effective validation. But the Baker and Snark have little systematic relevance beyond the narrow confines of the fictitious yarn in which they appear. They do have an attenuated relevance to much besides, through the mediation of Carroll's well-earned reputation for clever, whimsical writing. It is thus relevant, for example, to very important doctrines about the creative power of human thought and the criterion of coherence itself, of which the poem as a whole gives excellent illustration within its imaginary little universe of discourse.

A doctrine of God who is a Creator and Redeemer has

relevance of some kind to every reality and, indeed, every meaning which can be thought by one of His creatures. The believer in such a doctrine ought to welcome, then, the critical examination of it in relation to any and every human experience. Every illumination which the doctrine of God throws upon experiences of mathematics, humorous poetry, natural law, moral struggle or beautiful music will serve to establish the doctrine so much the more firmly in the system of truth known to man. To be sure, the existence of God is in no way dependent on man's knowledge of it nor on his critical examination of it. But if the existence of God is to be known *to man* it must be known in relation to some other aspects of his experience. The broader and more various such discovered relations are, the more important the knowledge of God becomes for man and the broader the base of his certainty in that knowledge.

When a man who professes faith in God resents another's making a broad examination of that doctrine, he raises a suspicion regarding the real depth of his assurance. Are his propositions regarding the deity, like Carroll's teachings about the Snark, merely relevant to a circumscribed universe of discourse? Or is his religious faith a kind of tragic play in which he becomes deeply involved while he is an actor in it but which he knows will be mostly irrelevant or contrary to the experience he will confront when once the curtain falls? If the God in whom he believes is the real Creator of the real world and the present loving Father of all men, will not the believer rejoice in finding everywhere the evidences of His creatorship and His love? Will he try to persuade men who are doubters to stop examining and weighing the evidence? Will he not, rather, call upon them to look more widely and deeply? Will he not be eager to point out the signs they have missed and to interpret in better perspective the data which they have misconstrued?

But, it may be replied, there may be some single moment in which God reveals Himself so clearly that all other evidences pale into insignificance. A man searching for his wife, feared lost in the bitter cold on a mountainside, may cling to the evidence of this fresh footprint and that crude cairn until he suddenly sees her alive and well. Then all other evidence seems irrelevant to him, not because it really is irrelevant, but merely because he has such evidence now as to make all other worthless by comparison. May there not be such moments of communion with God as to make other evidence quite unnecessary?

Yes, there are such moments. When a person stands at such a mountain summit of experience he needs no other evidence. But what if a man has never stood in such a relationship? Will he be more likely to discover God in such communion by rearing, about his soul, narrow walls, and then weeping disconsolately over his lost condition? Or will he better say with the Psalmist, "I will lift up mine eyes unto the mountains"? Even though he must still ask, "From whence shall my help come?" so long as he continues to look widely and with high eagerness for the answer, he is likely soon to say with assurance, "My help cometh from Jehovah, who made heaven and earth." It was Jesus himself who said, "Seek, and you will find."

Moreover, even the believer who has encountered God in great, decisive, redemptive moments must still come down into the valley of everyday toil. Happy is he if he has learned to see about him the many signs of God. Such a person is twice blessed now, for every such evidence of God is also a reminder of the great moments when He has made His presence known with especially overwhelming power and beauty.

Possibly some may argue that God reveals Himself to whomsoever He will and that the searching for Him will not affect in the least His speaking the decisive word when it suits His own good pleasure. It would seem unworthy of Christian reverence to conceive of God as so indifferent to men's earnest search for Him. But even if we could accept the belief that He was so indifferent, it would not justify the revolters' strictures against men's persistent striving after truth by use of such open-minded reason as we have been examining. For if God's revealing of Himself depends simply on His own good pleasure, unaffected by our searching, then there is nothing to be lost by searching. On the other hand, there would be much to gain, even though we could think that neither conclusive revelation nor the soul's redemption would ever be furthered in the least by such inquiry. For by means of it we might, at least, become aware of many lesser truths, and we might come to believe that the God who has created all things and who loves us actually exists. Such a belief, explicitly related to many experiences of our common life, could be expected to exert a wholesomely cleansing, comforting and challenging influence. That this can happen is attested by the witness of countless persons who do not know the meaning of a decisive moment in divine-human encounter, but who do bear witness in word and life to the help given them by their belief in God. Then whether or not it happens that God, in His good pleasure speaks the conclusive, revealing word also, nothing will have been lost by the rational quest of truth, while much will have been gained. On the other hand, if the Scriptures are right in all their admonitions to "seek," "test" and "think," we may by our earnest search actually prepare ourselves, as He intended, for His higher revelation of Himself.

In any event it ought to be clear that there can be no conflict between the reason of comprehensive coherence and revelation. For any thinker committed to use this criterion of all-round coherence is under special obligation, when examining a doctrine, to take particularly careful account of any revelatory claims and their supporting considerations, which believers in the doctrine commend to doubters. If there is any revelation or any divine sanction or significance of any revelation which the philosopher of open coherence has not taken into adequate account, that failure may be charged to his irrational prejudice or ignorance, but it cannot be fairly charged against that very reason which required the consideration of every available evidence.

E. THE MUTUAL DEPENDENCE OF FAITH AND REASON

As the motto of *Philosophical Fragments*, Kierkegaard quotes Shakespeare's observation, "Better well hung than ill wed." It is wise to observe this warning when seeking in practice to match faith and reason. Many a bad match has been made, in the history of theology, between faith and inadequate types of reason.

Only a reason committed from the start to leaving no relevant consideration out of account is adequate to be linked with faith. But such reason has already been joined with faith by the creative act of God. What God has joined together man must not seek to put asunder. Neither can live without the other. When either ignores its dependence upon the other, it does so at its own peril.

When faith is relied upon without the giving to reason of its just due, faith is in danger of becoming either a meaningless surge of emotion, a frenzied and senseless activity, or a thoughtless and violent attachment to unworthy ends. In either case, whatever significance it may retain is due to some rational structure which endures within it despite the irrational intention of the believer. In short, faith without reason is at best fanaticism and at worst insanity.

On the other hand, as we have previously observed,

reason is quite helpless without faith. What, then, is the proper way to think of the relation between the two?

What is needed seems clearly to be not more reason and less faith, as some overcautious philosophers have maintained. The tragic fanaticisms which have destroyed so much of value in human history have not been due to too much faith. They have been due to the separation of faith from reason. When men who have enough faith to act decisively are committed to irrational ends, while men of reason stand in faithless paralysis, catastrophe results. It seems certain that the world cannot be saved from its sorry plight by men of much reason but little faith. Only daring commitment and wholehearted action can make sufficient impact upon the world to stand any chance of significantly influencing its course. Men of intense and courageous faith are clearly needed. Too many people of high ability and sound ideals stand outside the decisive battles of life. The revolters, addressing thoughtful readers who, for the most part, already give assent to Christian ideals, have been quite right in insisting upon more faith and not less.

On the other hand, it seems equally clear that the need is not for more faith and less reason. In this direction there is either a blind rushing about in the shallow or perverted activism which the irrationalists so deplore or an inward withdrawal from all responsibilities in world affairs. Fanaticism and escapism cannot save either the individual or society.

What is needed is both more reason and more faith, combined in the same people.

Specifically, reason needs to be more loyal to its own principle of perseverance in examination of all experience. Too often the human thinker has fixed his attention simply on some particular kind of experience or some particular method of interpreting it and so missed entirely too much truth which would otherwise have been available to him. The need is for reason more broadly grounded in the total experience of men. It would seem highly advantageous, also, if more of the powers which God has given to man might be directed to the search for truth about man's own duty and destiny. The devotion of reason to puzzles in abstract, and ever more abstract, logic has provided a highly sophisticated pastime for many philosophers and in itself has been an intellectual good. However, while such great resources have been devoted to these puzzles, the urgent problems of discovering those ideal ends for which man exists and the resources by which he may have some chance to attain them have gone too often neglected. The rightful object of reason's attention is the whole truth. While analysis is useful as a stage in the discovery of that object, the obsession with the fragmentation of experience into minute and isolated elements has become a vice of the modern world. Often, in our time, the thinker abstracts from great segments of experience most important to him as an existing, purposive being, and then forgets that he has performed this act of self-abnegation and so falls into the absurd conclusion that such a being as himself could not possibly exist.

Autonomous human reason, independent of influence from nonhuman sources, is an abstract fiction worthy of the scorn heaped upon it by the irrationalists. The search for even the most infinitesimal core of reason of this kind is a quest for a will-o'-the-wisp, as the logical positivists have demonstrated. From beginning to end, reason is a part of a total experience, and man, though active in his experience, is not the author of it.

Hence, the attempt to escape from all fear and hope, ugliness and beauty, sin and righteousness, while a man withdraws into an ivory tower to think through the issues of faith, is doomed to failure. There is no seventh heaven so high nor Hades so low, in all our earthly experience, that a man can there find escape either from the world or from God.

It was while under the influence of such a false dream that a student once came to me for counsel about the method of reaching her philosophical goal. She had long been a religious believer. Now certain doubts had arisen. She was determined to have the truth and the truth alone, with no wishful thinking nor flight from reality. Should she not, therefore, leave off going to church, restrain herself from all attempts to pray, and keep away from her devout friends for a few months, while she thought these questions through to a conclusion? Only one answer can be given to such a person. By all means, let her close every channel of influence from the spiritual world, if she can, on condition that she take care to cut herself off, with equal thoroughness, from the material world. To refuse food for the soul but to feed the body would be simply to load the balance of evidence on one side. An artificially materialistic experience would lead naturally to an artificially materialistic philosophy.

Human thinking never takes place in an experiential vacuum. He who would reason with proper balance and a suitable objectivity must think, not in a vacuum but in a plenum.

It is true that the man who would learn the voltage of a lightning bolt may deliberately overlook all irrelevant data, while using instruments designed to bring him facts on this one problem alone. Such deliberate temporary impoverishment of experience is the price of those abstract truths sought by the specialized empirical sciences. But the man who would learn the truth about the purpose and destiny of his being and of the world must seek it not in maximum poverty but in maximum wealth of experience. Not the reason of mere analysis and bare abstraction, but the comprehensive reason of coherence must be his instrument.

Such reason is no foe of revelation. A thinker who is obeying the demand of coherence for consideration of all possible data relevant to his problem cannot ignore the most revealing impacts of God's activity upon himself and upon human history. To be sure, he will want to have evidence that they are revelations of God before he gives them central place in his thought and life. He will not accept every revelation-claim as veritable revelation. But neither does anyone else.

A believer in the method of coherent reason will probably be more likely to recognize and accept a true revelation than will others of equal endowment and opportunity. This is true for two reasons.

First, such a method requires him to look for new light everywhere and at all times. Whenever he closes the windows of his soul in arrogant finality he has lost both the humility demanded by his methodological principles and also the humility of true religion. The farewell to pride and the adoption of the eager, learning, venturesome spirit of the growing child whom Jesus set before us as an example will be mightily aided by the disciplines which must be learned in a steadfast search for truth consonant with all the data. "Oh send out thy light and thy truth; let them lead me,"[26] will be the continual prayer of the truth seeker who adopts the reason of comprehensive inclusiveness and catches a glimpse of the God in whom alone is perfect harmony. True revelation is less likely to escape his attention and open-minded consideration than it would be if his method did not require such constant and eager search for more light.

Moreover, he has an advantage in having at hand an instrument for distinguishing true revelation from false.

[26] Ps. 43:3.

He has a way of obeying the admonition to "test everything; hold fast what is good."[27] However inadequate may be his individual powers, at least he has a principle for "rightly handling the word of truth."[28] With such a critical instrument he will be less easily duped by every fanatic or impostor from without and every upsurge of repressed impulse from within. Of each revelation-claim he will ask that it aid in giving to thought and life a more comprehensive and harmonious meaning.

This was the method we observed John Knox to be using, even while he professed to condemn all efforts at proof of immortality. With him, we appeal to coherence in support of many a doctrine and commitment of the Christian faith, as we ask, "And yet what sense does the world make, what meaning can be found in human life without it?"[29]

This is the reason used in effective search for truth everywhere. Whether a man seeks the solution of a mystery story, the answer to a problem in algebra, the geological explanation of a coal deposit or the proper evaluation of another's conduct, what he wants is a conclusion which will make sense in relation to all the relevant data. But when he is dealing with a mystery story, algebra or geology, he is working with a specially designated area of experience deliberately abstracted from the rest of life. Hence, the relevant data to be considered are limited. On the other hand, the range of materials relevant to the evaluation of

[27] I Thess. 5:21.
[28] II Tim. 2:15.
[29] See pp. 32-33.

conduct is much broader and less clearly defined. Consequently, if the student of ethics limits his view, he does so at the peril of missing just the data most important to his solution. Even more, a problem concerning the destiny of man and the world requires the utmost possible catholicity of view, for no experiences are altogether irrelevant to such a problem, even though some are far more significant than others.

When the comprehensive reason of this kind is directed to the study of the New Testament, many uniquely valuable clues to reality are found there. The sweet reasonableness of divine love and mercy shines through the pages of the New Testament with a greater brilliance the more critically it is examined. Its message is wonderful beyond comparison. To the earthbound mind of the naturalist it may seem beyond belief. "And yet what sense does the world make, and what meaning can be found in human life without it?"

The revelation of truth to be found in the pages of Scripture is not, however, given for its own sake. God has not revealed the truth to us merely in order that we may know the truth. Rather it is that by knowing the truth we may be free from selfishness and falsehood; from the sins which do so easily beset us and from the narrowly circumscribed limits of our earthly existence.

Not that this earthly life is to be despised. The material limitations of our present world constitute the forms in which the eternal fellowship of the spirit is molded. To a large degree the character of the spiritual life we fashion here, both within ourselves and in community with others, depends upon the earthly institutions and material conditions through which we bring our spirits to bear upon one another. The effort to understand and to control our material environment must not be minimized. Rather, both our science and our common life must be wholly dedicated to God.

Even so, in a world fraught with constant peril, where both individuals and the race are threatened with death, can peace be found? Must the heavens, even, reflect the turmoil and uncertainty of earth? Can no absolute security be discovered among all the confusion and conflict of our time?

So long as sin and ignorance remain, our noblest visions and surest thoughts seem bound to be infected with the sense of our own limitations. The higher the ideal of supreme Good, the more restless is the dissatisfaction with our present moral state; the more exacting the ideal of perfect Truth, the more poignant our sense of the uncertainties and incompleteness in our own systems of knowledge.

Yet before the bar of reason itself, both the moral and the intellectual dissatisfaction bear witness to our divine heritage. We have been made for perfection and nothing less can satisfy us, but perfection is not yet ours. In this divine Word spoken within us is the ground both of our insatiable restlessness and of our reasonable, steadfast hope.

To be sure, man's reason alone will never find certainty

nor man's will alone ever discover the place of peace. For there is no such thing as human reason and will standing alone. In the grateful recognition of our dependence upon God and the dedication of our all to Him is the way that leads home. In such a consecrated life the divine image is continually renewed in us by His grace, while His spirit bears witness with our spirits that He is and that we belong to Him.

To the pilgrim whose reason and will are alike devoted to the service of God, the witness becomes clearer as the days pass. For "the path of the righteous is as the dawning light, that shineth more and more unto the perfect day."

The theoretical division of reason from faith produces the barrenness of logical positivism on the one hand and uncritical dogmatism on the other. The practical separation of reason from faith gives rise to a science devoted to the uncontrolled, amoral development of techniques for mass destruction and to a religion of fanatically intense feeling with no means of self-criticism nor of application to the tasks of our common life. Only by the union of reason and faith in the service of God can we hope both to know the Truth and to be free. For God is the ground of our reason, the source of our knowledge and the only hope of our salvation.

Index

213